✳ ✳ ✳

How Does Olive Oil Lose Its Virginity?

✳ ✳ ✳

Also by Bruce Tindall and Mark Watson

Did Mohawks Wear Mohawks?:
And Other Wonders, Plunders, and Blunders

* * *

How Does Olive Oil Lose Its Virginity?

* * *

Answers to the Enigmatic Questions of Contemporary Life

Bruce Tindall and Mark Watson
Illustrations by Cathy Dugan

QUILL / WILLIAM MORROW / NEW YORK

Library of Congress Cataloging-in-Publication Data

Tindall, Bruce.
How Does Olive Oil Lose Its Virginity? /
Bruce Tindall, Mark Watson.
p. cm.
Includes index.
ISBN 0-688-12681-2
1. Curiosities and wonders. I. Watson, Mark. II. Title.
AG243.T443   1994   93-49362
031.02—dc20   CIP

Printed in the United States of America

First Quill Edition

1 2 3 4 5 6 7 8 9 10

BOOK DESIGN BY CAROLINE CUNNINGHAM

Contents

Contents

Contents

CONTENTS

CONTENTS

CONTENTS

Introduction

How Does Olive Oil Lose Its Virginity? *answers questions about all* sorts of things you've always wondered about, and maybe even a few you haven't.

In this book, you'll take a trip around the world: observe an exorcism in Japan, ride camels in Kirghiz, and go on a head-hunting raid in Ecuador. You'll also travel through time and meet some famous and legendary people. You can pick apples with Eve and discover fire with cavemen; in modern times, you can share a chocolate bar in the Arabian desert with General Norman Schwarzkopf, and meet Aunt Jemima and Dr. Pepper.

There's a zoo in these pages, from huge elephants to tiny chiggers. You can soar with birds or dive to the ocean depths with sperm whales.

Some of the chapters let you explore your own body, from the hair turning gray on your head down to the smelly soles of your feet. You can learn about old and new cures for what ails you, too, from hiccups to sleepwalking. And if you just want to feed your face, our menu ranges from rare Chinese delicacies to Pennsylvania Dutch headcheese, with advice on avoiding poisonous mushrooms and iffy oysters.

Your journey can include not only other lands but even other worlds. After going Down Under to toss a boomerang and meet the Tasmanian devil, we'll take you *way* down under to find out all about demons, imps, succubi, gremlins, trolls, and ogres, as well as their friendlier cousins like nixies and pixies and hamadryads.

And if you've been itching to find out all about mosquitoes' optomotor anemotaxis, you've come to the right place.

Why Are Train Cabooses Red, and What Good Are They?

In the early days of railroads, everything, not just cabooses, was red. Red paint was cheap, so railroad companies bought it in bulk and swabbed it on all their train cars and buildings as well, according to John B. Buffalo, veteran of half a century of railroading and now with General Electric Railcar Services Corporation. Red paint also made trains more visible at crossings.

These days, however, not all cabooses are red. "Burlington Northern's are green; Chicago and North Western's, CSX's and Union Pacific's are yellow; and the old Chicago, Burlington and Quincy's were silver," says J. Donlan Piedmont of the Norfolk Southern. The traditional red, however, is still predominant.

The car that brings up the rear, the caboose, has served many functions. According to Piedmont, "In its Golden—or Red, if you like—Age, the caboose was home and office to train crews. It had a stove, bunk beds, a bathroom of sorts and a desk where the conductor could handle all the paperwork." The crew kept tools in an underslung cellar or "possum belly" beneath the car. On cattle trains, the stockmen rode in the caboose.

Caboose crews had some dangerous jobs. In the old days, says Buffalo, "the brakes on the engine were minimal and on descending grades the engineer could not control the train. The train crew would mount the tops of the cars and set hand brakes to avoid a derailment caused by [excessive] speed."

The caboose protected the train in other ways as well. The engineer could make sure the train was still intact by glancing behind for flags or lanterns hung on the sides of the caboose. Crewmen in the caboose watched for dragging equipment and other problems that might cause a derailment. Also, dispatchers and switchmen watched for the caboose so they could be certain that the whole train had passed a critical point. That was vitally important on a single track shared by trains running in both directions. For example, an eastbound train couldn't move onto the track until the westbound train had cleared. If some cars of the westbound train had accidentally become uncoupled, the absence of the caboose would warn the switchman that the tail of the train was still blocking the track.

The word *caboose* existed long before railroads. Originally, it meant a shack where sailors could cook their meals, built on the deck of a ship too small to have a full-scale galley. According to George R. Cockle of the Union Pacific, the railroad caboose began similarly, around 1850, as a cabin built on a flatcar. The cupola, or lookout, was added to the top of the caboose in about 1863. Later, as taller freight cars came into use, the high-riding cupola was replaced by bay windows on either side. The crew watched from these lookouts for problems with the rest of the train, and signaled from them to the engineer. In the 1950s, cabooses were outfitted with two-way radios, and by the 1970s, some of them even had seat belts.

"The days of the caboose are numbered," says Buffalo. Electronic devices can monitor the tracks for problems that could cause derailments. Computers do much of the paperwork. Crews sleep in motels. "For good or bad," laments Piedmont, "nostalgia ain't what it used to be."

Not all cabooses served such workaday purposes as tool storage or brake setting. The Orient Express of the 1880s had a caboose called a fourgon, carrying food, champagne, a refrigerator, and all the trimmings for the passengers' luxurious three-hour-long dinners.

Railroaders have a variety of other names for the little car at the end of the train. Some are dull (*van, waycar*) but many are picturesque: *bazoo wagon, brain wagon* (because the conductor, boss and brains of the crew, works there), *crumb box* or *crummy, louse cage,* and *strawberry patch* (because of its traditional red color and the red lanterns displayed at night).

Sodbusters—homesteaders in the wilderness of Canada— had cabooses, too, even though they didn't have railroads. They traveled in wood-and-canvas huts perched atop sled runners, and called the contraptions *cabooses.* When the homesteaders staked their claim, they took the caboose off the skis and transformed it into a house—sort of the Great White North version of the mobile home.

How Are Condoms Electronically Tested for Reliability?

Condom manufacturers provide more choices—ribbed, colored, extra-large, ultra-thin, extra-strong, even flavored—than Madonna can find ways to use them. But one thing we've noticed that they all seem to have in common is the packaging statement that the condoms have been "electronically tested for reliability." How, we wondered, is this done? Further investigation also revealed that the packaging for the so-called natural (non-latex) condoms warns: "Not for use in preventing sexually transmitted diseases." So what's the thrust of all this?

We posed these questions to Bradley Pugh, vice president for Scientific Affairs at Aladan Corporation, makers of Gold Circle brand condoms (so named because they're distributed in brightly colored foil packages in the shape of a coin). He had the following titillating response:

Condoms are 100 percent electronically tested (in the United States, at least)! All American manufacturers use either a wet or dry electronic test on 100 percent of the product before it is packaged and distributed. This is how it's done:

Wet Method: The dry condoms are stretched over a metal form (usually some percent larger than the condom in order to assure that the film is stretched tight). The condom-coated form is then submersed in a water bath, and an electronic circuit checks for the presence of holes by measuring resistance between, or electrical current flow between, the water bath and the metal form. Since the latex rubber from which the condom is made is a good insulator, if there is no hole, current does not flow, and resistance is high.

Dry Method: This method is very similar to the wet method in principle. A condom is also placed over a metal form, but instead of immersion in a water bath, the condom-coated form passes under a conductive net, or over a conductive pad. The system is charged with a relatively high voltage (about one thousand volts) and if there is a hole, the electric charge will pass through the hole to the metal form, where an electrical circuit detects the presence of a hole and causes the condom to be rejected.

Following either of these methods, inspections are performed at random in order to insure that the electrical circuits are functioning as they are supposed to. This inspection involves filling the condom with three hundred milliliters of water and observing for leaks.

Natural or "skin" condoms are made from the cecum of lambs (part of the intestines). These are cleaned and finished off by applying an elastic band, or drawstring, to the top. This is necessary because skins don't have the memory or elasticity of natural latex and therefore tend to be somewhat larger and need securing on the penis. Tests have indicated that some of the smaller organisms that can cause sexually transmitted diseases (STDs), like hepatitis B virus, *may* be capable of penetrating the skin membrane, leading the U.S. Food and Drug Administration to suggest that these be used as a contraceptive only.

It has been estimated that less than 20 percent of the persons worldwide who should be using condoms for hygienic reasons actually use them. These simple devices, which have been around for many years (perhaps thousands, as there is some evidence the ancient Egyptians used penile sheaths made of papyrus),* function both as an effective contraceptive and STD barrier. It is believed that if used consistently and correctly, condoms alone could make a serious contribution toward alleviating the AIDS crisis.

On a lighter note, the ancient Egyptians supposedly also used a vaginal contraceptive suppository made with crocodile dung. Perhaps this was an effective population-control method not for contraceptive reasons but because of the risks of obtaining the crocodile dung, given the general disposition of the creature.

---

* James S. Murphy, *The Condom Industry in the United States* (Jefferson, N.C.: McFarland and Company, 1990).

✳ ✳ ✳

How Does Grecian Formula 16, Which Is Clear, Color Gray Hair?

✳ ✳ ✳

The hair coloring product Grecian Formula 16, manufactured by Combe Products Inc., is applied every day until your gray hair matches the color of your base (non-gray) hair, then two or three times a week to maintain the color. Since the product is a clear liquid, how does it dye the gray hairs? And why doesn't it make your base hair darker and darker, leaving the gray hair to "chase a moving target?" Before answering, let's review some basic hair facts.

All *mammals* have hair, but hair is lacking in all other taxo-nomic classes with the possible exception of some prehistoric reptiles. On some mammals, the hair is very sparse, notably whales (which have bristles around the mouth), elephants, rhi-noceroses, walruses, and an herbivorous aquatic order of mam-mals known as the sirenians. This order includes Steller's sea cow (a beast of up to twenty-six feet in length, which seal hunters literally ate into extinction a few decades after its discovery in 1741); three species of manatees; and the dugong. (Manatees and dugongs are similar creatures: Both are torpedo-shaped with two flat flippers in front, no hind limbs, and a wide horizontal swimming tail that's rounded in the manatee, but forked in the dugong. The dugong's snout is turned downward, and the male's incisors grow into tusks as they mature. The manatee has the curious distinction of having six neck verte-brae, instead of the seven present in all other mammals. These animals sometimes suckle their young by holding them upright with a flipper so they can reach the mammary glands in the pectoral area. It's been speculated that this unusual feeding position may have been the genesis for the myth of the mer-maid. Both populations have been severely depleted by hunters, who slaughter them for meat and oil.)

There are several specialized forms of hair. A rhinoceros horn is actually a dense aggregation of fused hairs. Porcupine quills are a special adaptation of hair, and all mammals except man have a form of hair that acts as a touch-sensitive organ—the *vibrissae*. These stiff hairs, which have sensory nerve fibers at the base, comprise the whiskers of a cat; are located around the mouth of a dog; on the abdomen of a squirrel; and on the wrists of those small, wide-eyed, monkey-like critters called lemurs.

Human hair takes three forms. As early as three months into gestation, the fetus develops a downy hair all over its body that falls out prior to and shortly after birth—the lanugo hair. Hair grows inside tubular indentations in the outer layer of the skin (epidermis) called follicles, and by the sixth month of gestation, the fetus has its full lifelong supply of them. After birth, the child begins to grow villus hairs, which are short, fine, unpigmented, and found all over the body except the palms, bottoms of the feet, and in between the fingers and toes. (If you hold your hand up to a light and look across the back of it, you'll see villus hairs). All other hair—body, scalp, and axillary (pubic and armpit hair)—is called terminal hair, and shares a common structure.

The base of the follicle is bulbous, and ringed by *matrix* cells, which form new hair cells (which die shortly thereafter) primarily composed of the protein *keratin*. These cells form the hair shaft, which has a spongy center called the *cortex,* a tubular inner layer of elongated, attached *medulla* cells that provide strength, and an outer layer of *cuticle* cells, which overlap like roof shingles. (The three-toed sloth exhibits a remarkable symbiotic adaptation: A microscopic alga that grows on the cuticle cells spreads its coat with gray and green hues that provide the sloth with camouflage in the forest canopy.) One's natural coiffure is governed by the cross-sectional shape of the hair shaft: Straight hair is round, wavy hair is elliptical, and tightly curled hair has a flattened configuration. (If you think *you* have "bad hair" days, be thankful you're not one of the few dozen people diagnosed with the rare malady "uncombable hair syndrome." Their hair shafts have odd shapes, for example, triangular, and even copious amounts of hair conditioner fail to untangle them.) Attached to the side of each follicle is the *erector pili* muscle, which contracts in response to cold (or fright) to pull the sloping hair shaft upright, creating a "goose pimple" in the process. When humans were far more hirsute, this created a raised mat of hair that trapped an insulating layer of air—a function that's now vestigial. Also attached is the sebaceous gland, which lubricates the hair with oily *sebum* as it emerges from the follicle.

There are between one hundred thousand and one hundred fifty thousand terminal hairs on the scalp, growing about half an inch per month. Each hair has a growth (*anagen*) phase of two to six years after which growth slows to a halt over a few months in the *catagen* phase. The *telogen* phase sheds the hair (there are between thirty and one hundred hairs shed from the scalp daily), and the follicle restarts hair production from scratch. Lifetime hair production per follicle is about twenty-five feet, cumulatively.

Let's dispel some common myths about hair.

You cannot turn gray overnight in response to stress or some frightful experience. Hair is dead protein, and there is no mechanism that would extract the pigment (melanin) from your hair overnight.

Cutting hair does *not* make it grow faster. There are two factors that may contribute to this widely held misperception. First, hair *does* grow faster in the summer, so people who cut their hair more frequently during this season for comfort in the summer heat may notice this misleading correlation. Second, people who cut their hair short and then grow it long may be deceived by the *relative* decreases in the length of hair growth over time. For example, suppose you cut your hair to a length of one inch on January 1, and it grows one-half inch per month. On February 1, it will be an inch and a half long, an increase in length of 50 percent. On March 1, it will be two inches long, an increase of 33 percent over its length on February 1. On April 1, it will be two and a half inches long, a mere 25 percent increase over the month before, and so on.

Another myth is that hair continues to grow after death. This is impossible, since the productive matrix cells are dead, and the hair shaft is dead cells to start with. The confusion may arise because skin shrinks somewhat post mortem, possibly causing the follicles of facial hair to retract, leaving a mask of protruding hair stubble in an area that was previously clean shaven.

If you're struggling with baldness (alopecia), be thankful you can turn to the drug minoxidil (originally used to treat hypertension) or a good hair weave, and don't have to sample some of the ancient treatments. An interesting book* describes one early Greek and two early Egyptian treatments. The Egyptians tried a potion made of dates, dog toes, and asses' hooves, as well as a preparation made from the fat of a lion, hippopotamus, crocodile, cat, snake, and goat. The Greeks toyed with boiled live viper broth—talk about "snake oil" medicines! And if you've ever cured a hangover with "the hair of the dog that bit you," note that the phrase relates to an old superstition that a dog bite should be treated with burned hair from the hostile canine.

Now, to the crux of our concerns: hair color, Grecian Formula 16 (GF16), and that pesky, creeping gray. We spoke with Dr. Herbert Lapidus, who is director of research and development for Combe Products Inc. (and, coincidentally, the inventor of Combe's Odor-Eaters Insoles, but more on that later). He graciously solved the mysteries for us.

In each hair follicle bulb there are pigment-producing cells— the *melanocytes,* which pump melanin into the hair shaft. Red hair acquires its color from red melanin; the other colors, blond to brown to black, derive their color from successively larger concentrations of black melanin. A hair becomes gray when its melanocytes die or drastically reduce their melanin production. While GF16 is 98 percent clear liquid, there's a small amount of yellow sulfur that tends to gravitate to the bottom of the

---

* Doug Podolsky, *Skin: The Human Fabric* (Washington, D.C.: U.S. News Books, 1982).

bottle and should be mixed in by shaking prior to application. The liquid contains lead acetate, which coats and is absorbed into the hair shaft. The acetate chemically reacts with natural sulfur *inside* the hair shaft to produce a dark pigment. It also reacts with the sulfur deposited on the *outside* of the shaft to similarly darken the shaft exterior, so you get color inside and outside the shaft, permanently attached (until the hair grows out and falls out in the telogen phase). The treatment is repeated daily until the gray hair matches the base hair. GF16 *does* color the base hair slightly, but for the most part, the natural melanin in the base hair occludes the GF16-derived pigment, so there's no moving color target. Dr. Lapidus pointed out that the dyed gray hair probably never matches the base hair *exactly,* but that scalp hair is always a blend of various shades, so the result looks natural.

Fine, but what about redheads? Dr. Lapidus said that someone with blazing red hair who wanted to maintain that appearance might not be satisfied with GF16—it would produce a red-brown blend, which is a tone that redheads tend to acquire naturally as they age.

In the course of our conversation with him, we discovered that Dr. Lapidus invented Odor-Eaters Insoles, and has the dubious distinction of carrying the titles of chief odorologist and judge at the Odor-Eaters International Rotten Sneaker Contest, held in Montpelier, Vermont, every spring. Contestants (under age eighteen) who have won regional contests come to Montpelier from all over the world to compete for the title of World Champion and prizes including: A five-hundred-dollar U.S. savings bond; a year's supply of Odor-Eaters products; sneakers (or *trainers,* as the British call them) for the whole family; a Purple Sole of Valor for the mother; and enshrinement of the winning (maximally grotesque) sneakers in a glass case known as the "Hall of Fumes." The shoes are judged on stench (the

British call this *pong*), sole, lace, Velcro, eyelet, grommet, toe, and heel degeneration, "tongue fatigue," and overall "squiffiness."

We asked Dr. Lapidus what causes foot pong to vary among individuals, and he said the main variables are sweat production and shoe composition, which affect the *real* cause of foot odor: bacterial growth. There is also a condition called bromhydrosis, which afflicts 5–10 percent of the population, causing them to secrete sweat that stinks even *before* bacteria go to work on it.

We wondered what "activated charcoal" is, the effective ingredient in Odor-Eaters Insoles, and learned it means ground charcoal that has been superheated in an anaerobic environment to produce scads of fissures in the granules. This results in a huge total surface area for the charcoal—about the size of a football field for a single pair of Odor-Eaters! The molecules that generate shoe pong bind to the charcoal because it's electrically charged, a process called adsorption. Activated charcoal is also used to trap radioactive elements in nuclear power plant coolant water, and it's present in airport ceilings to remove noxious jet fumes.

Finally, we couldn't help but ask Dr. Lapidus if he really did sniff the squiff of Odor-Eaters contest participants. He said: "If it's a particularly bad shoe odor, I know it before I put it to my nose." Furthermore, he stated unabashedly: "Odor is a very important part of our lives and it's a great way to differentiate. And if you didn't have any odor, Mark, you wouldn't enjoy any food. So, you gotta take the good with the bad. By smelling sneakers, I get to eat good food!"

* * *

Why Is There a Sperm Whale but No Ovum Whale?

* * *

S*exism under the sea? Well, no. The sperm whale's name comes from* the mistaken belief that the economically important white goo found in its head and other parts of its body was in fact what the substance's name implies: *spermaceti,* Latin for "sperm of the whale." Spermaceti is definitely not sperm. It's now thought to be either part of the whale's echo-location or "sonar" equipment, or else a cushion that helps the whale survive when diving as deep as three thousand feet.

Spermaceti has been used as a medicinal ingredient for hundreds of years. Old medical texts prescribed such preparations as spermaceti with red wine, spermaceti with mummy (exactly what it sounds like: pulverized mummies), and spermaceti with fresh egg yolk. It was also used to make candles. Sperm oil, derived from spermaceti, was used as a lamp oil and as a high-pressure lubricant in machinery, especially in the textile industry.

Sperm whales—Moby Dick was one—can be as large as sixty feet long. They travel in herds of fifteen to twenty, although individual males sometimes travel alone. They have teeth, unlike some species of whales that feed by straining ocean water through a sieve-like structure called a baleen. Oddly, though sperm whales use their teeth to catch large fish and squids, they don't use them to chew. The prey is just swallowed whole.

A whole, unchewed squid contains a sharp, knifelike piece of cartilage called the beak, down the middle of its body. Squid beaks can irritate the whale's digestive tract, causing the intestine to secrete a substance that apparently surrounds the annoying object and alleviates the pain. Eventually, the whale expels this stuff, which when fresh is soft, dark, and stinky, but with exposure to sea water and air becomes waxy, lighter in color, and more pleasant-smelling.

This substance is called ambergris, another valuable whale product, but not at all the same thing as spermaceti. It's an important fixative used in making perfume (a Chinese term for ambergris, *long xian xian,* means "fragrant dragon-spit"), but the seventeenth-century English considered it a breakfast delicacy, too. Milton's *Paradise Regained* contains a reference to "gris-amber steamed."

Originally, ambergris was called *amber,* and the prehistoric hardened tree resin that we now call amber was called *yellow* amber. But eventually, to avoid confusion, the whale ooze got the name ambergris, French for *gray* amber.

* * *

What Happened to Ford's Models B Through S?

* * *

*F*ifteen million of the legendary Model T automobile rolled off Ford Motor Company's assembly lines from 1908 to 1927, and the Model A is almost as famous, although it was produced for only three years, from 1928 to 1931. But was there any rhyme or reason to the cars' names? Why did the A come *after* the T, and what happened to all the letters in between?

There *was* a Model B (there were two completely different cars named Model B, in fact); there *was* a Model S; and there were several letters in between. The very first Ford cars, though, didn't have model designations at all.

Henry Ford and his wife, Clara, tested his first homemade engine in their kitchen sink on Christmas Eve, 1893; he drove his first completed car out of his workshop shed on June 4, 1896. (He had to knock down a wall first, to the landlord's great consternation, because he hadn't planned ahead. He later placated the landlord by replacing the missing wall with the world's first garage door.) He subsequently sold this car, the "quadricycle," for two hundred dollars.

By 1899, several wealthy Detroit businessmen had invested in Ford's first car-manufacturing company, but it made only about a dozen automobiles, referred to today only as Ford's "second car," "fourth car," etc., and was not a financial success. That wasn't unusual; car companies were being founded and going out of business all the time around the turn of the century.

Ford spent the next few years building racing cars, which won numerous competitions and attracted public attention. Two cars he built in 1903 were named the 999 and the Arrow, although they were identical; one of them was the first automobile to break the one-minute mile.

With this experience, success, and publicity under his belt, Ford went back into the business of manufacturing cars in quantity. The Ford Motor Company, organized in 1903, sold two or three thousand copies of its two-cylinder Model A, and enhanced models, called the AC and C, during that year and the next. This early car should not be confused with the other, more famous Model A, which came out a quarter of a century later.

Meanwhile, Ford's partner, Alexander Malcomson, had been pushing the development of an upscale car, which emerged as the two-thousand-dollar Model B in 1904. The expensive, four-cylinder B didn't sell very well, which was fine with Henry Ford; unlike many carmakers, he was interested in making a lot of inexpensive vehicles rather than a few costly toys for the rich.

Ford followed the A and B with other models in alphabetical order, although a few letters were skipped. (No one really knows what happened to models D, E, G, L, and the rest of the unused letters. Cathleen Latendresse of the Henry Ford Museum thinks they probably were prototypes that never made it into production.) The mid-priced F and fancy K models were followed in 1906 by the affordable Model N, and its slightly more deluxe cousins, Models R and S. The N was Ford's most successful model to date.

By 1908, Ford was making one hundred cars a day. In the few years since the turn of the century, the number of automobiles in the United States had grown from eight thousand to one hundred forty thousand. But the car that automotive historian Beverly Rae Kimes says "brought about a revolution in the mode of American life" was Ford's next design—the Model T, introduced in 1908.

The Model T, colloquially known as the Tin Lizzie or flivver, was durable, cheap, and easy to maintain. The owner could make repairs with string and other household items; there was an old joke about the hardware-store owner who took down his old sign, JUNK OF ALL KINDS, and replaced it with one reading FORD MOTOR PARTS. At first, buyers could select from Model T's in red, green, pearl, black, and French gray, but when mass production started in 1914, Ford discovered that there was only one kind of paint that dried fast enough to keep up with the pace of the assembly line—giving rise to the saying, "You can have any color you like, as long as it's black." (New paint technology allowed the reintroduction of other colors in 1926.) The Model T came in many different shapes and sizes, though, including a basic economy version, a pickup truck, and a fire engine. All of them, however, had the Model T motor and other design elements in common.

The Model T proved itself and captured the public imagination by winning a 1909 New York-to-Seattle race (in twenty-two days, mostly over poor or nonexistent roads), and was a favorite for many years. Despite some drawbacks—it ran noisily and didn't handle bumps in the road very comfortably—buyers snapped up Tin Lizzies at prices that went down from $850 in the first year to $290 by 1924. But in the mid-twenties, Ford began to lose market share to other companies with newer designs.

At first, Henry Ford stubbornly refused to change the Model T, but eventually realized that after almost two decades, it was getting pretty long in the tooth. Ford was interested in a new eight-cylinder "X engine," but the design wasn't far enough along to put into production. Instead, during 1926 and 1927, Ford engineers designed a completely new four-cylinder car. Ford decided to break the tradition of alphabetical order and call it the Model A, apparently, according to historian Kimes, "to allay suspicions it might be a revamped Model T,"* which could have arisen if it had been called the Model U. (Ford's foreign subsidiaries did make some on-beyond-T cars in England and Europe, such as the Model Y of 1933, according to Walter MacIlvain of the Veteran Motor Car Club of America, but none was marketed in the United States.)

The Model A had a forty-horsepower engine that could easily run at sixty-five miles per hour and was quieter than the Tin Lizzie. Many features that were available only as costly options on other cars were standard on the Model A, such as hydraulic shock absorbers and safety glass.

---

* Beverly Ray Kimes, *The Cars that Henry Ford Built* (Princeton, N.J.: Princeton Publishers, 1978).

Ford made the Model A for three years, then followed it with another four-cylinder car, the Model B, once again reusing an earlier model's moniker. Kimes calls it "the Ford nobody noticed." It lasted only one year, 1932, and sold only about a quarter million copies. Henry Ford had lost interest in four-cylinder engines and was working on a V-8, which he introduced in 1932 in the Ford Model 18—the 8 standing for the number of cylinders in the engine, and the 1 indicating that it was Ford's first V-8. This new type of car could start quickly and run at up to eighty miles per hour, making it popular as a race car among stock-car drivers, and as a getaway car among such notorious customers as Bonnie and Clyde.

The almost invisible 1932 Model B was the last of Ford's letter-designated cars. The 18 was followed by other numbered models such as the 40, 48, 68, 78, 81A, 82A, and the last model introduced before Henry Ford left the company in 1945, the 11A.

What Should You Do When a Stutterer Gets "Stuck"?

*W*e've all experienced it. *The guy in the next office is a stutterer, and* he comes in your office to ask you a work-related question.

You say, "Hi John!"

He replies, "Hi. If you've g-g-got a minute, I need some help, p-p-please."

"Sure, what's up?"

"The c-c-c-c- . . ."

He seems to be stuck or hung. It's only a few seconds, but

you're both rapidly becoming uncomfortable. You want to be helpful, if you can, or at least not hurtful, but you don't know what to do. You decide to just smile reassuringly—but hold on! What if he thinks you're smiling *at* him? OK, you'll just maintain eye contact and wait—but what if looking directly at him is making him uncomfortable? All right, you'll look away—oh, no! Maybe he'll see that as impatience. Aha! You've got it. You know what he's trying to say!

"The computer is down?"

He shakes his head. After a short pause, he says, "The copier needs toner."

Now you feel like a clod. You're *both* a little embarrassed, and the sad irony is that it's not really anybody's fault. So what *should* you do (or *not* do) when a stutterer gets stuck? And why do people stutter anyway?

Prolonged stuttering strikes 4 percent of all children (25 percent of all children experience a short-term stuttering phase), and 1 percent of all adults. There are many techniques that stutterers can use to improve their speech, and indeed, there are (and have been) many famous people afflicted with stuttering whose identities would probably surprise you. According to the National Stuttering Project (NSP),* they include: Aristotle, Winston Churchill, Isaac Newton, Erasmus Darwin, Charles Darwin, Marilyn Monroe, Somerset Maugham, Lewis Carroll, Clara Barton, King George VI of England, Charles Lamb, Virgil, Aesop, Moses, Raymond Massey, Neville Shute, John Updike, Mel Tillis, Bob Love, James Earl Jones, Bruce Willis, Carly Simon, and Annie Glenn. John Stossel, one of the hosts of the popular TV show *20/20,* recently revealed on that program that he, too, is a stutterer.

---

* National Stuttering Project, 2151 Irving St., No. 208, San Francisco, CA 94122-1609.

(Incidentally, you may recall that in the hit comic movie *A Fish Called Wanda,* actor-comedian Michael Palin of Monty Python fame played a stuttering buffoon named Ken, a both humorous and disquieting role. Before he is assailed for insensitivity, it should be noted that he helped found the Michael Palin Center for Stammering Children in London, England, partly in homage to his father, who struggled with the problem.)

Stuttering (or *stammering,* as the British call it) is also known as speech dysfluency, but the organizations we contacted apparently accept the term *stuttering.* The NSP, however, encourages people to refer to themselves as a "person who stutters," rather than "a stutterer," because it is something one *does,* rather than something one *is.*

There are two classes of stuttering: acquired and developmental.

Acquired stuttering is the result of some trauma such as stroke, accident-induced neurological damage, or severe psychological incident.

Developmental stuttering usually starts in childhood between the ages of three and six, and gradually progresses. Since it runs in families, it may be genetic. Developmental stuttering, like the acquired variety, may have a neurological component, and there is some evidence of reduced blood flow to the brain—but it's definitely *not* "simple nervousness." Interestingly, estimates are that boys are five times as likely to be stricken as girls. This is the same sex ratio exhibited for some other neurological disorders such as: dyslexia—a reading disability in which the person has difficulty discerning the order and orientation of letters in a word (for example, *was* is read as the word *saw,* and the letter *d* is seen as *b* or even *p*); dysgraphia—an inability to write; and Tourette's syndrome—a disorder involving involuntary movements and head jerks, and sometimes curious vocal tics such as grunts, barks, and spouted obscenities. According to

Hugo Gregory, director of stuttering programs at Northwestern University, it is very important to note that early intervention can prevent prolonged stuttering in about 95 percent of all cases.

For reasons as yet unknown, most people who stutter are quite fluent when they speak in isolation, whisper, sing, speak in chorus, or when they can't hear their own voice.

So what should you do when you're rappin' with a person who stutters and he or she gets stuck (a phenomenon known as *blocking*)? The NSP, the Stuttering Foundation of America, and the American Speech-Language-Hearing Association all gave nearly identical advice:

* *You might be very tempted to finish sentences or fill in words for the person. Unless you know the person well and have his or her permission, please do not do this. It is assumed that you are sympathetic to the person's plight. More important, your action could be taken as demeaning. And, of course, if you guess the wrong word, the difficulties multiply.*

* *Refrain from making remarks such as "Slow down," "Take a breath," or "Relax." Such simplistic advice is not constructive.*

* *Maintain normal eye contact and try not to look embarrassed or alarmed. Just wait patiently and naturally until the person is finished.*

* *A person's stuttering sometimes makes it harder to understand what is being said. If you do not understand what is said to you, don't be afraid to say, "I'm sorry, I didn't understand what you just said." No matter how much of a struggle it is for the person to repeat it, it is preferable to your pretending you understood, or guessing what his or her communication was.*

* *Be aware that people who stutter usually have more trouble controlling their speech on the telephone, so be extra patient*

in that situation. If you pick up the phone and there's si-
lence, it may be someone who stutters and is having trouble
initiating the conversation.

* Speak in a relaxed, unhurried manner, and pause slightly
before beginning, but don't make your speech unnaturally
slow.

* People sometimes wonder if they should ask a person questions about his or her stuttering. That is something that
must be left to your judgment. But surely, stuttering should
not be a taboo subject. If you have a question about it, the
person will probably appreciate your asking. It is in your
mutual interest that it be talked about openly. You should
be prepared to find that some people who stutter will be
sensitive about it, but if you follow the rules of common
politeness, there should be no problem.

* In general, let the person know by your manner and actions
that you are listening to what he or she is saying and not
how it is being said. Be yourself. Be a good listener.

There are various techniques that are known to improve some
people's fluency. Throat-muscle tension may be a factor in
stuttering, and biofeedback therapy is sometimes used to teach
patients to keep those muscles relaxed. Some programs attempt
to teach control of the larynx in terms of the rates of vocal cord
opening and closure, as well as the tension of closure. Many
teach a reduction in overall speech rate, which can be very
effective but may produce a monotonous delivery. Sometimes
a stuttering block can be broken by a diversionary tactic on the
part of the stutterer, such as slapping a desk or tapping a foot.
The drawback is that the effectiveness tends to wane as the
novelty wears off, and the person may be left with the distract-
ing action as part of a blocking complex. Some people who
stutter try to think a few phrases ahead while they're speaking
in order to avoid certain words that they know cause them a
problem, giving them time to formulate easier substitute words.

Unfortunately, the distraction and complexity involved in this approach can be self-defeating.

Herb Goldberg, president of the Foundation for Fluency, recommends an antiblock technique he calls pseudo-stuttering. When caught in a serious block, the person *deliberately* stutters the blocking word, unbeknownst to the listener, and thereby gains control of his speech and manages to "skate through" the rough word.

There are several devices available to aid those who stutter, but none is a cure, and in some cases, their effectiveness has not been fully demonstrated through carefully controlled studies. One is an electronic metronome that's worn like a behind-the-ear hearing aid, and produces a continuous set of evenly spaced clicks that reinforces the goal of maintaining a slow and even verbal pace. Another device is a throat microphone to pick up the person's speech and transmit it to him through a set of headphones, with a few seconds' delay. The delayed-speech transmission encourages (forces?) the speaker to maintain a slow pace. Finally, there is a device based on a premise previously mentioned—that people rarely stutter when they can't hear their own voice. This device has a throat microphone (strapped or taped on), and a set of clear plastic ear molds, all of which are attached to a small sound generator clipped to the user's clothing. When the user speaks, his voice is masked out entirely by a buzzing sound. A recent British study of 195 subjects showed an 89 percent reduction in stuttering with this device, and 82 percent of the study participants reported "considerable" improvement with it.

In addition to phone conversation, we found from our research that certain social situations are particularly prone to evoke angst in a person who stutters. Some involve dealing with clerks and other service people who must take customers' orders and are in a hurry to do so. Ordering in a restaurant, because it is so public, with an unfamiliar waiter or waitress pressed for time, seems to be one of the worst. The following joke has made the rounds among people who stutter and is offered here, not for its humor, but for the insight it gives into the compromises that pervade the lives of people with a stuttering problem:

"What would you like on your salad?" said the waiter.

"R-r-r-r-roque . . . r-r-r-ro-r-roque . . . I'd like to try the r-r-r-r-r-roque . . . I'll have the Thousand Island."

What Makes
a Rattlesnake's
Rattle Rattle?

We contacted the Department of Biology at the University of North Carolina (UNC), and Dr. Mel Turner at Duke University, and posed this and other puzzles to them regarding snakes.

Our UNC contact's response to the title question was:

Rattlesnake rattles are sets of specialized scales [from] the tips of their tails. Every time that the snake sheds the outer layer of its skin, that special scale [on the tip segment] is left behind, sort of wrapped around the next remaining version of itself. You may know that all snakes shed the outer layer of their skins every few months, more frequently in proportion to how fast they are growing. In rattlesnakes, the shed parts of this one set of scales are specially evolved to stay behind, one around the next, so that each snake has as many rattles as the number of the times it has shed its skin, less any that have accidentally been broken off.

The purpose of all this is to scare away big animals from

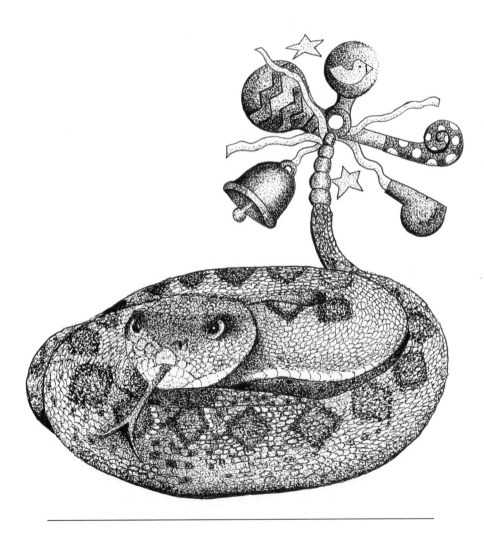

stepping on them, or other animals from bothering them. Lots of kinds of snakes also rattle their tails in the leaves, or wherever, as a warning. They don't want to bite you and will avoid it any way they can. Biting something big is apt to hurt their teeth, maybe even fatally for them if the injuries get infected. Copperheads do this; so do blacksnakes. But they can't make as good a noise as a rattlesnake, some of which can sound like industrial warning buzzers. [Dr. Turner told us that the rattling noise comes from the fact that when the tail tip is vibrated, the loosely attached rattle segments rub against one another; there's nothing *inside* the rattle banging around.] The total number of snake-bite deaths in the United States per year usually runs about a dozen, most of which are in zoos or [among] other people keeping exotic snakes. Religious fanatics "taking up serpents" used to cause another three or four deaths per year, with our dear Durham, North Carolina, being the national center for this sort of thing (no kidding). [The authors live near Durham—*ouch!*] If copperheads or rattlers bite someone many times, one bite right after another, it can be fatal. One bite rarely is—probably never in a healthy person. It is basically a little less serious than a broken leg. The only things in our woods that can kill you are ticks and myopic hunters.

Now we know how rattles form and make noise, but can you deduce a rattlesnake's age from the size or number of rattle segments? According to Dr. Turner:

You cannot tell a snake's age in years by its rattle, but I should qualify this. A new segment is added every time the snake sheds its skin. Snakes shed a few times a year (this varies, and changes), and eventually, the terminal part of every rattle breaks off, so you can't [deduce] too much. On the other hand, the very first rattle segment of a baby rattlesnake is distinctively shaped (the "button"), and the rattle segments of young, actively growing snakes become successively larger, so a small snake with just the button is a newborn, and a snake with a strongly tapering series of segments is a young one. Conversely, a snake with a rattle showing little or no tapering has lost the early formed part of its rattle, and has been adult at least the time it took to grow the extant portion.

OK, so we're rattlesnake experts now. We also asked: Do cobras really spit? And, do Indian snake (cobra) charmers really exist? Dr. Turner replied:

Do cobras spit? Yes, some species of cobras do "spit" or spray venom from their fangs as a defense. More than one kind of cobra does this, in Africa (a couple of species) and Asia (some races of the Indian Cobra). They face their attacker with mouth opened slightly and eject two streams that become a spray that can reach several feet, and high enough to reach the eyes of a person. The venom is very irritating to the eyes, and can cause blindness if not washed out quickly. The same species can also bite in the usual (much more dangerous) way. They bite their prey, but spray venom at their enemies' eyes.

Do snake charmers exist? Well, yes, and no. There are people in India and elsewhere who display snakes for the public, but the snakes aren't really "charmed." First, snakes are nearly deaf—they don't hear the flute or whatever. The spread hood and erect posture is the defensive display of an unhappy cobra, so they aren't tame animals. I suppose some may have been defanged (or have had their mouths sewn shut—animals are cheap), but for the most part, as I understand it, the snake "charmers" just have a good sense of the snake's behavior, and guide [its] motions without getting bitten. The defensive snakes sway in time with the charmer because they are alertly following his motions as a possible threat, not because they are dancing to the music. [The charmer] stays just out of range. (Actually, cobra strikes are supposed to be relatively slow.)

We continued our quest to solve the great mysteries of herpetology by asking the following: What's the difference between a boa constrictor, an anaconda, and a python? These are three humongous snakes that squeeze and suffocate their prey, and swallow them whole. So how do they compare in size, habitat, strength, danger to humans, and so on, and which one would win in a fight to the death? Dr. Turner came to the rescue:

All are related as members of the family Boidae. Popularly, "boa constrictor" has often been used for any giant snake, but strictly, it applies only to the species *Boa constrictor,* ranging in several races from southern Mexico to southern South America. (Incidentally, this is probably the most widely familiar scientific name of any species of organism!) The common boa is actually only a moderately large species; very large individuals of the largest races (South American) are about ten to twelve feet, and often are mature at much smaller sizes. Habitat: ranges from tropical forest to open, rather arid country. Food: probably mostly rat-sized—small mammals, birds, etc.

Several related genera are also called *boas.* Many of these include much smaller species, two of which occur in the western United States. Some boas are burrowing types, others are terrestrial or arboreal. Most "boas" are New World, a few are in Madagascar, some on certain Pacific Islands, and some of the little burrowing types are in Africa and Asia.

Anacondas are giant, semiaquatic boas of tropical South America. The big one is *Eunectes murinus,* the green anaconda (there is also the smaller yellow anaconda, *E. notaeus*). Maximum size estimates I've seen for the anaconda vary from about twenty to more than thirty feet: It is easily the largest snake in the New World and probably the world's largest—[specifically] in terms of mass—since anacondas are very heavy-bodied animals. A nineteen-foot (pregnant) anaconda weighed 236 pounds, according to [snake researcher] C. H. Pope. Again, there is a wide range of what may be considered normal adult sizes, and probably anything much over seventeen feet is a big anaconda.

Pythons include a few genera and numerous species of

snakes (most often treated as subfamily Pythoninae in the family Boidae). Pythons differ from boas mostly in technical ways: One notable difference is that pythons lay eggs, whereas the boas give birth to live young. (The boas and pythons are among the most primitive snakes in various ways—they still have two lungs—one is lost in more advanced families—and they still have hind legs! The legs are visible as small claws or spurs on either side of the vent; they are usually larger in males and are used in courtship.) Only a few of these species are giants; many are moderate-sized or small snakes. With one possible exception (*Loxocemus,* a modest-sized Mexican-Central American snake which perhaps does not belong in this group), all pythons are Old World species concentrated in Africa, Australia, Southeast Asia, and islands of the western Pacific. The reticulated python, *Python reticulatus,* is probably the longest snake in the world, and has reportedly been measured exceeding thirty-two feet. Again, this is an exceptional size, and any python much over twenty feet is very large. The reticulated python is relatively slender compared with the anaconda (or to a lesser degree, the other big python species). A healthy twenty-two-footer may weigh about 225 pounds, but longer ones can weigh less [according to researcher C. H. Pope]. . . .

[*Python molurus bivittatus,* the Burmese python, is reported to reach twenty-five feet.] Again, eighteen feet would be quite large. The African python, *Python sebae,* can also exceed twenty feet, but is usually less than fifteen or sixteen feet. The Amethystine python, *Liasis amethystinus,* ranges from the southern Philippines to Australia, and apparently rarely exceeds twenty feet, but is usually much smaller. It is relatively slender. There are a few other largish (ten feet or more) pythons, but these seem to be the biggest ones.

Your other boa/python questions: relative strength, danger to humans. All are large, strong snakes. Large individuals of the largest species could be dangerous. Large wild pythons have been captured with leopards in their stomachs! Captive pythons, though usually fed smaller animals, have eaten animals as large as an eighty-four-pound goat [again, according to C. H. Pope]. Wild ones often eat such things as deer, antelopes, wild pigs. It would be extremely unusual, however, for a wild python or anaconda to attack a human in an attempt to eat him. There have been isolated reports of *wild* pythons having killed people. It is almost impossible for a snake to swallow a normal-sized person (the shoulders are too wide) but I know of a single, very old, report of a fourteen-year-old boy killed and eaten by a large reticulated python. The same case has been repeatedly cited, which illustrates the rarity of the event.

Constricting species of snakes generally restrict the constricting behavior to capturing prey. When defending themselves they may strike repeatedly and bite without trying to constrict the attacker. Bites by large pythons and boas can inflict painful wounds (but no serious danger). (Of course, when capturing one you would have to wrestle the body as well as having to control the head and teeth.)

Boa constrictors and Burmese pythons are commonly kept as pets and often (not always!) become very tame, although the latter's eventual great size makes them difficult to keep. Reticulated pythons, anacondas, and some other species are reputed to be more prone to bite. Some snakes are reported to get cranky as they get larger.

The real danger from giant snakes involves feeding-time accidents and careless owners of captive snakes. People have on rare occasions been killed by *pet* pythons, probably because the animal was excited and confused by the odor of food animals on or near its owner. Snakes are not bright creatures, and odor is more important to them than vision. They may try to constrict a person if he smells like a rabbit to them. Therefore, one should not handle the snake's food (or any other animal) before handling the snake, and one should be cautious when handling even the tamest big python. Always have another adult present. (Although I have heard that an attacked person can often unwind a big snake, provided his arms aren't pinned, a person attacked by a two-hundred-pound or larger snake would probably be unable even to stand for long.)

Mostly, however, it's the snake that is in danger from humans. Many of the big snake species are overexploited for leather, for meat, or for the live animal trade, and some are threatened or endangered species.

Which would defeat the others in a fight? The fight would be staged, presumably, in captivity. The outcome would depend on the animals' relative size, motivation, luck. Most of these aren't especially snake eaters (some smallish Australian pythons are). Anacondas do eat [many] other things—caimans (alligatorlike creatures) and (young) crocodiles, so I wouldn't be surprised if one ate a boa. Pythons also eat some reptiles. If you were to rub one with food, another might attack it, but I don't know what you'd prove. Probably the biggest one or (if same size) the one that first managed to wrap up the other in its coils would win.

Finally, in his letter, our UNC contact addressed a commonly held belief we hadn't thought to ask about, and made a truly impassioned plea for a change in people's attitudes toward serpents:

Your letter with the snake questions has been passed along to me, apparently because I am the one who gets to identify the various innocent snakes that citizens have moccasins and then bring us for confirmation that they are water mocassins, copperheads—and worse. Practically none of them are copperheads, although the few that *are* are usually alive and contained tenuously in cracked mayonnaise jars with rocks on the lid! One of the questions and answers that you might consider including in your next book is "whether you can reliably tell the difference between poisonous and non-poisonous snakes by the arrowhead shape of their heads." The answer is, "Not really." Lots of nonpoisonous snakes have [heads just as wide] as any copperhead. Plus which, there are some poisonous ones with narrow heads. Coral snakes are the best example. People should be encouraged not to kill any of them, and not to expect my praise when they do. . . .

Anything you can do to help the public become less fearful and fixated on snakes, fearing them and killing them at every opportunity, would be a public service. It would help avoid so much needless fear and worry, and also save the lives of a lot of harmless animals that people could and should be enjoying as much as so many people do wild birds. A ringneck snake is as handsome as any cardinal, as easy to identify unambiguously, and even less likely to hurt you.

Why Is
Dr Pepper
Soft Drink
Named That?

Before we get to that, a moderate digression: We wrote to several beverage companies and public-health officials seeking the truth about an expression that both of us, and some of our friends, had heard many times in our childhood: "The last 10 percent of a canned or bottled beverage is 90 percent backwashed spit" (this having been a common response to an attempt to pilfer the drink of the guy next to you). Was (or is) this a nationwide expression? Did it originate as a line from a comic movie? Is it an actual fact derived from epidemiological studies of drink-sharing as a vector for saliva-based diseases?

Alas, we're stumped and humiliated. George Charalambous of the Anheuser-Busch brewing technical services department chided us with:

"Insofar as what you call a 'common belief' regarding drinking directly out of a can or bottle [is concerned], we cannot believe that this is a serious statement in the first place, therefore the question cannot be taken seriously either. We don't want to comment further."

Oh, the indignities of being pioneer researchers! George, being a basically good-humored fellow, however, ended his letter with: "P.S.: This writer always pours his beer in a glass."

Then there was Jim Ball, vice president of corporate communications for Dr Pepper/7UP soft drinks, who seemed to suggest that we had a region-based problem with our swallowing methodology. He wrote:

"You've certainly picked a subject unknown to me. This 'backwashed spit' phenomenon must be endemic to the Cary region [which is where the authors live]. I'm not sure what 'backwashed spit' is, or what it means."

How'd this guy get to be a vice president? He continued: "While not a physicist, I don't think spit can rise into a vessel that is higher than the point of flow entry. Wouldn't spit flow down a throat that is in a position of incline in order to accept the downflow of a liquid?"

In other words, depending on whom we talked to, the question was either unanswerable, stupid, or moot. If any of our readers out there don't agree, we'd love to hear from you.

Serendipitously, Mr. Ball thought we might be interested in some corporate literature which, coupled with some additional research, answers this chapter's title question. But first, some background.

The Dr Pepper and 7UP companies merged in May of 1988. The parent company, through its subsidiaries, also markets Welch's brand soft drinks, as well as IBC (Independent Breweries Company) root beer and cream sodas, and their diet equivalents. IBC root beer was introduced in 1919 as an alternative to alcoholic beverages during Prohibition, acquired a substantial market in many cities, but subsequently fell off in popularity after World War II. It has, however, made a comeback since the 1970s. In 1990, the Dr Pepper subsidiary introduced the Nautilus thirst quencher which was, at the time, the only sports drink sweetened exclusively with aspartame. All told, the parent company is the most prolific producer of noncola soft drinks in the world, and the third largest maker of soft drinks overall.

Dr Pepper is named for Dr. Charles Pepper, the owner of a drug store in the town of Rural Retreat, Virginia. Dr. Pepper had a young daughter who became romantically involved with a pharmacist named Wade Morrison, who was working in the store. Dr. Pepper quashed this budding affair, and Morrison split for Texas, opening Morrison's Old Corner Drug Store in Waco. Charles Alderton, an Englishman working the pharmacy and doubling as a soda jerk at Morrison's store, was the person who synthesized the prototype soft drink, in 1885, from various fruit flavors. Morrison liked it, the customers liked it, and one informed patron jokingly suggested it be named after Morrison's love interest's father (a little brown-nose action if ever there was any!).

Eventually, the two entrepreneurs couldn't manufacture enough syrup to meet demand from other soda fountains, so they contacted Robert Lazenby, owner of The Circle 'A' Ginger Ale Company. Lazenby modified the formula somewhat (he was a beverage chemist) and began making the syrup, finally bottling it as well after collaborating on further formula changes with Morrison. Amazingly, in the interim, Alderton, who spawned the product in the first place, relinquished any claims on the drink (the dolt!).

The 1904 World's Fair Exposition in St. Louis, attended by twenty million people, saw the world premier of several future staples of the American diet: Dr Pepper, ice cream cones, and hamburgers and hot dogs served on buns! The soft drink's market was expanding rapidly, so Morrison and Lazenby started the Artesian Manufacturing and Bottling Company, later to become the Dr Pepper Company.

Some of our readers may remember the Dr Pepper slogan, "Drink a bite to eat at 10, 2, and 4." J. B. O'Hara, a former president of the company, stumbled on some research in the 1920s or 1930s showing that most people experience a loss of energy during the day at about 10:30 A.M., 2:30 P.M., and 4:30 P.M. Sugar relieves this symptom, hence the slogan.

So how did 7UP get *its* name? The original 7UP was a caramel-colored lithiated lemon-lime soft drink invented by C. L. Grigg, who had formed the Howdy Company of St. Louis in 1920. The company's principal drink was initially Howdy orange drink, but that soon changed and so the company name was changed. The 7 in *7UP* comes from the heavily promoted fact that it is made from seven natural flavors. The origin of the *UP* moniker is anybody's guess, but perhaps it's because the sugar in the drink sets you "up." Certainly, the choice is preferable to "7Down" or "7Sideways"!

Some early 7UP slogans are rather amusing (to all but, perhaps, the FDA). For example, there's: "7UP energizes—sets you up, dispels brain cobwebs and muscular fatigue." As well as: "Fills the mouth—thrills the taste buds—cools the blood—energizes the muscles—soothes the nerves—and makes your body alive—glad—happy."

* * *

Are Some Individuals More Attractive to Mosquitoes Than Others, and If So, Why?

* * *

Research has solidly demonstrated that some people are indeed more attractive to mosquitoes than others. The attractiveness may vary over time, though. Within a group of people, one may get bitten more often than the others for a few days, and then someone else may get the honor for a week or so. The processes by which mosquitoes find and select their unfortunate victims, though, are so complicated that, despite decades of research, there's still no simple and well-accepted answer as to why. In 1971, University of Alberta entomologist (bug scientist) Brian Hocking wrote, "Rarely has so much work yielded so little consensus of opinion"* as in the field of mosquito attraction. The situation was the same twenty years later, when University of Wales biologist M. J. Lehane wrote, "Information on what signals are used and the processes involved is still fragmentary."** Lehane's book, which summarizes the current state of mosquito research, abounds in words like "unclear," "equivocal," and "unknown."

Research on mosquitoes (much of which is funded by the military) is complicated by the many different species of blood-sucking insects that exist, each of which has its own behavior patterns, and by the complexity and versatility of the insects' methods of searching for food. Between the time a mosquito is just sitting around to the moment it jabs its nasty little beak into your flesh it tends to go through three stages.

First, hunger causes the mosquito to begin a *general search*. It flies around, usually in a pattern likely to expose it to any interesting smells or sights that might be in the vicinity. This phase hasn't been studied much, but typically, the insect may fly crosswind in open country, in order to sample as many different airstreams as possible; or, in the woods, its strategy may be just to stay put and wait for a possible meal to walk by.

During the general search, the mosquito may encounter a stimulus that suggests that dinner is nearby. This begins the *activation* phase of its behavior, during which the insect orients itself toward a potential host.

Finally, when the mosquito is in the immediate vicinity of its target, it enters the *attraction* phase. At this point, various stimuli combine to make the mosquito decide whether to land on a specific individual (human, bird, cow, whatever).

---

* Brian Hocking, "Blood-Sucking Behavior of Terrestrial Arthropods," *Annual Review of Entomology*, 1971.
** M. J. Lehane, *Biology of Blood-Sucking Insects* (London: HarperCollins Academic, 1991).

To make things more difficult, it turns out that some stimuli that attract mosquitoes during one phase may repel them during another. For example, carbon dioxide (which mammals exhale) is an *activator,* helping the mosquito orient itself toward a target, but during the final *attraction* decision, CO_2 is a repellent.

Scientists have experimented with many individual chemicals found in breath or sweat. Frequently, these substances have little effect on mosquitoes when used in isolation, but do attract or repel when combined with one another. For instance, lactic acid plus carbon dioxide activates mosquitoes' orientation behavior more than carbon dioxide alone; but lactic acid alone has no effect. According to Brian Hocking, no specific chemical has ever been found to be as attractive to mosquitoes as a whole intact human being.

Mosquitoes have good eyesight, and visual clues are important, especially during the activation phase of the hunt. They seem to gravitate toward black, blue, or red colors (all of which they may see as black), and simple contrasts—such as a dark cow against a green field or light sky. Complex patterns, though, decrease attraction. Other blood-sucking insects, such as tsetse flies, have similar behaviors. A dramatic illustration of this effect is the fact that striped zebras are more prevalent than solid-colored ones in areas infested by tsetse flies. The tsetses are more likely to bite and fatally infect the solid-colored zebras, so the striped ones have an evolutionary advantage.

The mosquito's sharp eyes are connected to a brain which may be tiny but can perform what seem to be very sophisticated calculations. During its general search phase, for example, a mosquito needs to fly at right angles to the prevailing wind so as to expose itself to as many wind-borne smells as possible. Mosquitoes (just like birds, bats, you, and me) can't *feel* the direction of the wind unless they're standing still. But like airplane pilots, they can determine the wind direction while in flight, by using visual clues. If the mosquito is trying to fly straight ahead, but sees objects on the ground going by at an angle instead of directly from front to back, it "knows" that a crosswind is affecting its flight, and can make appropriate adjustments. This ability is called optomotor anemotaxis.

After being activated by visual and chemical clues to fly in the general direction of a possible host, the mosquito goes into its final attraction phase. Body heat and the resulting convection currents are important at this stage. Mosquitoes may fly toward cardboard cutouts that look like cows, but veer off when they get about one foot away from them and don't feel any heat.

One of the most important practical goals of this research is the discovery of effective mosquito repellents. Washing with soap and water is one possibility—it removes some of the chemical clues of your presence. Ingesting sulfur also works, but unfortunately, only if you take it in such high doses that it colorizes your sweat and repels fellow humans, too.

"Deet" (N, N-diethyl-m-toluamide) is a very effective repellent for mosquitoes as well as other pests. However, a 1990 study by U.S. Army researchers found that in *small* doses, deet actually *attracts* mosquitoes! So, if you've used a deet-based repellent, but find that you're beginning to get bitten as it wears off, you should either slather on a lot more, or else wash it off completely. However, Joe and Terry Graedon (of the People's Pharmacy books and radio program) warn against using large doses of deet on children, in whom it can cause convulsions.

The Graedons suggest a couple of other possible repellents that seem to work, although they apparently haven't been scientifically tested: swallow thiamine (vitamin B1)—about fifty milligrams for an adult—and lots of garlic. They say many people swear by Avon's Skin-So-Soft lotion, diluted with three parts water, for external use. This repellent, they claim, is especially popular among an unlikely bunch of Skin-So-Soft customers: the United States Marines.

*   *   *

Who Discovered Fire?

*   *   *

In our previous book, Did Mohawks Wear Mohawks? *we answered* the question, "Who invented the wheel?" It was pretty straightforward, so we thought we'd follow up with the obvious companion question: "Who discovered fire?"

The answer isn't nearly as simple. Wheels, connected by an axle and attached to a vehicle, don't occur in nature; some human being had to invent them. Fire, though, does happen naturally, as the result of lightning, hot lava, spontaneous combustion of coal deposits, or even sparks struck by rocks collid-ing in an avalanche. So even the earliest humans, and even their pre-human ancestors, had already *discovered* fire, in the sense of having encountered it. The significant questions, though, are several:

* *Who figured out that you could do useful stuff with fire?*
* *Who devised ways of carrying naturally occurring fire home and keeping it going?*
* *Who invented or discovered how to start a fire without hav-ing to rely on natural processes?*

Many cultures had myths about how people first got fire. These are usually "vivid dramas . . . few of them tame," wrote the late Walter Hough, head curator of anthropology at the Smith-sonian Institution. Hough noted that many such myths had to do with the *theft* of fire. He surmised that these myths developed in the earliest days of human use of fire, when no one knew how to make it, and possession of fire gave one group an advantage over another. Another group of fire myths explained how the gods had locked away fire in flint or other fire-*making* materials. As Hough pointed out, these latter stories could not have developed until after people had found ways to make fire at will.

A familiar Greek myth falls into the category of the earlier, theft-of-fire stories. Prometheus, one of the Titans, stole fire from Zeus and gave it to humans. In retaliation, Zeus subjected Prometheus to eternal punishment, and sent evils, toil, and disease to the mortals via Pandora's Box.

Today, anthropologists believe that humans had learned to control fire—that is, keep it burning over a long period of time—as long as a million years ago. Some of the evidence, though, is sketchy and controversial. For example, a cave at

Cho-k'ou-tien, China, was long thought to contain ashes from a controlled fire that had burned constantly for generations half a million years ago. But in the 1980s, anthropologist Lewis Binford began to question this conclusion. He thinks the ashes may be from spontaneous peat fires. Binford thinks that the Cho-k'ou-tien cave people probably did use fire to some extent, but doubts that they could preserve and control it as continuously as had previously been thought.

Other sites containing possible evidence of early controlled fires are in south China (about one million years ago), Hungary, and Spain (both about a half million years ago). In warmer climates, such as Indonesia and Africa, there is no evidence of controlled fire more than seventy thousand years ago, but researchers don't know whether that's because fire was less necessary there than in colder regions of Europe and China, or just because tropical climatic conditions are not as likely to allow charcoal to survive long enough for archaeologists to find it.

At any rate, some hundreds of thousands of years ago, people in various parts of the world managed to keep the home fires burning. Other important inventions that probably came later, but can't be dated with any certainty, were methods of transporting fire: for example, by carrying a torch; or, for canoe travel, by putting a clay plate on the boat floor, with gravel on top of it and embers on top of that; or, in the England of Shakespeare's time, by taking along a slow-burning "fusse ball" or puffball fungus.

People gradually discovered or invented refinements in the art of feeding and preserving fires. The choice of fuel can be important. Charcoal (which occurs naturally as the result of fires) ignites at 580 degrees Fahrenheit, as compared to pine wood at 800 degrees; loose grass or leaves are even easier to light. Coal wasn't used as a fuel until relatively recently: The Chinese were using it a thousand years ago or so to smelt iron—Marco Polo wrote about the "black rocks" they burned. The Hopi Indians independently discovered its usefulness several hundred years later. In some places, fuel is whatever can be found: for instance, in icy Greenland, gull guano.

The fireplace started out as a box of earth in the center of the house, with perhaps a hole in the ceiling to let the smoke out. Egyptians invented the bellows around 1500 B.C. Somewhere along the way, people discovered that andirons, holding the fuel off the floor and creating a draft, made the fire more efficient. Imperial Romans had the flue, a pipe or conduit to carry the fire's heat to another room. But it wasn't until the fourteenth century that someone created a fully enclosed furnace with a chimney.

The many methods that have been invented for striking or kindling a fire are impressive evidence of human ingenuity. The fire drill is a sharp stick spun back and forth between the palms of the hands or by other means, drilling into a piece of wood, generating both wood dust and sufficient heat to ignite it. Cultures all over the world (with the puzzling exception of Japan) invented versions of the drill. Other friction-based fire starters include the bamboo saw and the rattan thong, both from Borneo. Eskimos, Malays, and Europeans all discovered that flint and pyrites struck against each other would create a spark. Bamboo and a piece of pottery can produce a similar effect, as people from Vietnam to the Congo have found. Several different chemical means of starting fires, such as matches, were developed around the world. And the ancient Greeks used a glass lens to kindle fire directly from the sun, especially when they needed "pure" fire for religious ceremonies such as the Olympic Games.

Even more diverse than ways of making fire are the uses to which people have put it. You can keep warm by sleeping next to the fire, of course. But the Cocopa Indians, who lived by the

Gulf of California, found a more efficient way of keeping warm without having a fire burning constantly all night: They built a fire on the sand, let it go out, then covered themselves with a blanket of warmed sand. Less obvious is fire's usefulness for cooking, which must have been discovered by accident, perhaps when some meat fell into a fire. (After all, who would have imagined that a yummy chunk of raw bear meat would taste even yummier if you burned it a bit?) Fire can be used not only to cook food, but also to catch it in the first place. People all over the world have deliberately set fires to flush animals out of cover and toward hunters—animals from buffalo and hyenas to grasshoppers and termites—as well as to repel predatory animals from a campsite at night. The use of smoke to repel insects is almost universal.

Ancient Native Americans, as well as fifth-century B.C. Kurds, used both the light of fires and smoke signals to communicate; pre-Columbian Mexicans built fire-illuminated lighthouses on the coast. Native Americans also used fire in lieu of tools for many purposes, including woodworking (from felling trees to carving canoes), as well as for shaving: Instead of using a metal blade, Sioux men singed the hair off their faces.

All of which is very interesting, but none of which really answers the question of who first discovered fire. Unfortunately, nobody knows.

* * *

Who Was the Model for the Statue of Liberty?

* * *

According to one legend, the sculptor's mother was the model for Lady Liberty's face, and his wife was the model for the rest of the statue. (Paging Dr. Freud!) The sculptor Frédéric-Auguste Bartholdi was aware of this legend and never denied it, but he never confirmed it, either. Other stories had it that the colossal lady with the torch resembles the widow of sewing-machine inventor Isaac Merrit Singer, or some anonymous Parisian model.

The story that Bartholdi's wife was the model for the statue's body is almost certainly untrue. He first met Jeanne-Emilie Bocheux de Puysieux in America in 1871, but didn't see her again until 1876, by which time he had not only designed the statue, but had actually produced the right arm, hand, and torch (which were displayed at the Centennial Exposition in Philadelphia that year). So she could not have posed or modeled for the statue.

For the same reason, Mrs. Singer could not have been the model. She didn't meet Bartholdi until his work on the statue was well under way. Besides, posing as a sculptor's model *just wasn't done* by respectable ladies of the upper and middle classes.

It's not altogether impossible, however, that the intense, determined face on the statue was inspired by that of Charlotte Bartholdi, the artist's mother. A resident of Alsace, Mme. Bartholdi refused to leave her home even after the region was occupied by Germany following the Franco-Prussian War of 1870–71. Photographs of Mme. Bartholdi's face do reveal a resemblance to the statue's. Bartholdi could have patterned Liberty's face after his mother's both as a tribute to her courage in refusing to give up her home to the Germans, and as a symbol of French resistance to the occupation. That wouldn't be the only association the Statue of Liberty has with French politics of the 1870s.

The idea for the Statue of Liberty was born in a conversation between Bartholdi and statesman Edouard de Laboulaye in 1871. Emperor Napoleon III, a dictator who had run France as a police state for almost twenty years, had been overthrown at the end of the disastrous Franco-Prussian war. Laboulaye and others who wanted to restore democracy and human rights sought to repair French relations with the United States, which had been damaged by Napoleon's support for the Confederacy during the American Civil War. They hoped that the American republic would be a good example and ally to the newly freed French republic. One part of their friendship campaign would involve gifts to the American people, including two statues by Bartholdi—a likeness of Lafayette, the French general who helped Americans win their Revolutionary War, and the Statue of Liberty.

But these French republicans were no French revolutionaries. They were moderates. Many of the symbolic details of the Statue of Liberty contrast sharply with those of art in the decades just after the French Revolution of 1789. Instead of carrying a firebrand for use in burning down the enemy's positions, the lady in New York Harbor carries a torch to shed light. In her other hand, instead of a gun, she holds the tablets of the law. Her feet trample a broken chain, symbolic of liberation from tyranny, but the chain became less and less prominent in successive designs of the statue, and in the finished version is hardly visible under her sandals and the folds of her robe. Instead of the cylindrical cloth "Phrygian cap" or "Liberty cap" symbolic of revolution, she wears a crown radiating seven beams of sunlight, representing the light she sheds on the seven seas and the seven continents (and also representing the sculptor, whose family coat of arms included a sun emitting seven beams).

Even the title of the sculpture and the materials from which it is made are symbolic of moderation and peace rather than revolution and violence. "Liberty Enlightening the World" hardly sounds like a call to arms. Her exterior is made not of melted-down enemy cannon and ammunition, like many triumphal victory statues, but rather of copper, "the fruit of labor and of peace," as Laboulaye put it. Many of the symbols in the statue are Masonic as well—enlightenment, the sun, the law—for Bartholdi was a member of a Masonic lodge.

We know much about how the idea for the Statue of Liberty

came about; we know much about its symbolism. We know that Gustave Eiffel is responsible for pulling off the great engineering feat of actually constructing the full-scale statue, that editor Joseph Pulitzer led the campaign to raise money for the statue's pedestal (and that Governor Grover Cleveland vetoed a New York State appropriation for that purpose), and that Emma Lazarus wrote the poem, "The New Colossus," inscribed on it. But the name of the model or models is still a mystery. One book* suggests that Bartholdi deliberately refrained from revealing this, and encouraged speculation, to increase public interest in the statue. But, its authors say, it's possible that the statue actually depicts a woman known to posterity only as Céline, who picked up a few extra francs modeling for artists when she wasn't walking the streets of Pigalle, Paris's red-light district.

* Christian Blanchet, Bertrand Dard, Bernard A. Weisberger, *Statue of Liberty: The First Hundred Years* (New York: American Heritage, 1985).

What
Causes
Déjà Vu?

Didn't we just answer this question? No? We must have been suffering from what Saint Augustine, sixteen centuries ago, called false memories, and has also been called paramnesia, memory illusion, double perception, false recognition, and many other terms.

Charles Dickens's character David Copperfield called it "the strange feeling to which no one is quite a stranger." That's something of an exaggeration; various studies have found that as many as 96 percent to as few as 30 percent of the people surveyed said they had experienced déjà vu. It seems to occur more often among the young and the better-educated, but with equal frequency among both sexes. People who have had déjà vu experiences tend also to have had feelings of depersonalization (the dreamlike feeling that one is observing one's own actions, that one is not one's self) and word alienation or semantic satiation (the phenomenon in which a word seems to lose its meaning when repeated over and over).*

There is no official definition or recognition of déjà vu in the American Medical Association's standard reference book, the *Diagnostic and Statistical Manual*. But psychiatrists and psychologists have put forward many definitions over the years, including this typical one: A "subjectively inappropriate impression of familiarity of a present experience, with an undefined past." The *subjectively inappropriate* part is important: You feel that you've been in this situation before, yet the logical and rational part of your mind tells you that you can't possibly have been here. This cognitive dissonance between what you feel and what you know gives déjà vu its eerily confusing effect.

Many explanations and theories of déjà vu have been advanced over the years, and none is universally accepted. Here are some:

* *Believers in reincarnation think the memory may be a real memory from a past life.*
* *Sigmund Freud thought that déjà vu during a dream represented a desire to return to the mother's genitals or the womb—a place where the dreamer actually has been before.*
* *Freud also suggested that the current situation could be similar to an unconscious wish or fantasy.*

---

* See the chapter "Repetition, Repetition . . . Huh?" in our previous book, *Did Mohawks Wear Mohawks?* (New York: Quill, 1991).

* *Followers of Freud theorized that the déjà vu experience was a way of reassuring oneself that a threatening situation would turn out all right in the end.*

* *Déjà vu could be a disorder of memory and perception. The mind has been likened to a tape recorder, with "recording" and "playback" heads. If the wires get crossed (literally or figuratively), you could think you're remembering something that you are in fact experiencing and "writing" into your memory for the first time.*

* *It could be the conscious recognition of a sight, sound, or other stimulus that was unconsciously perceived a few seconds before.*

* *The current situation could be similar to a barely remembered dream.*

* *Current and past situations could have been similar though not exactly the same, and just as two different pictures seen through blurry glass might look the same, the two experiences might feel the same. A refinement of this theory, by Dutch researcher Herman Sno, uses analogies between the brain and holography and other information storage and retrieval technology.*

* *An organic (physical) problem in the brain could cause it. Brain surgeons have been able to induce feelings of déjà vu by electrically stimulating certain locations in the temporal lobe. And many people have reported feelings of déjà vu as part of the "aura" that surrounds the onset of an epileptic seizure, though studies differ on whether déjà vu is any more frequent in epileptics than in other people.*

The term *déjà vu* (French for *already seen*), coined by the French philosopher E. Boirac in 1876, has inspired a long list of other *déjà*'s, including *déjà lu* and *déjà entendu* (already read and already heard—used in unfavorable book and music reviews), *déjà rencontré* (already met), and *déjà goûté* (already tasted).

* * *

Why Do
Camels Have
Humps?

* * *

*H*umps *help camels survive in the harsh desert environment, but they* are not storage tanks for water. In fact, according to zoologist and camel expert R. T. Wilson, camels don't store large amounts of water in their stomachs or anywhere else, either. After a camel has drunk its fill, its body is about 70 percent water—about the same proportion as a cow, a human, or any other land mammal. Rather than storing extra water, camels survive long periods without drinking by conserving the water in their bodies.

Nevertheless, camels do sometimes have to sweat in order to cool down, and that's where the hump comes in. Most of a camel's fat is concentrated in the hump, rather than being spread out more evenly over the whole body as in other animals. A layer of fat interferes with the ability to sweat, so by keeping most of the body fat-free, the camel is able to sweat over most of its body surface. This increases the cooling effect of perspiration.

But sweating to cool down is a last resort. The camel's body has other ways of dealing with heat that don't involve loss of water, and it uses those first before putting the sweat glands in gear. A camel's normal body temperature can fluctuate by 6 Celsius degrees without ill effect. (The equivalent in a human would be a temperature that could vary between 93 and 104 degrees Fahrenheit and still be considered "normal.") If the camel had to maintain a more constant temperature, it would have to sweat out an additional gallon and a half of water every day.

Camels' bodies also conserve water by concentrating their urine, which contains more salt and waste matter and less water than that of other animals. Their intestines also reabsorb most of the water from their feces.

Some camel behaviors, too, help them conserve water. When they lie down, for instance, they face the sun, so that the heat falls on the smallest possible surface area, rather than on their broad sides. And while some animals cool off by breathing rapidly, camels don't because they would lose too much water vapor in their breath. A panting dog can breathe three hundred times a minute, but a camel's respiration rate, even when hot, is only about twenty.

It would be possible for the camel to convert the fat in its hump into water, but the amount of energy it would take to do that would cause the camel to breathe so heavily that it would lose more water by exhaling than it would get from the fat, so in practice this conversion does not happen.

Because most of the fat is stored in the hump, the meat of the rest of the camel is relatively low in fat and high in protein. Suet made from hump fat can be stored for up to three years. The Gabbra people of Kenya castrate camels so they will develop even fattier humps, then use one camel's fat for an entire family's cooking needs for a whole year.

Everything we've said so far has to do with the one-humped camel, or dromedary (from the Greek word meaning *to run*), which lives in hot climates. There are also two-humped, or Bactrian, camels, named after the region where they live (ancient Bactria, or modern-day Afghanistan and surrounding areas), but relatively little scientific research has been done on them.

Camels evolved from an American animal, Protylopus, which was rabbit-sized and lived during the Eocene epoch (roughly forty to fifty million years ago). It's not known whether this forerunner of the camel had humps or not; since there is no hump bone, it's impossible to tell from a skeleton alone whether an animal had two, one, or no humps. Protylopus's descendants still extant in the Americas include llamas, alpacas, and vicuñas, none of which has humps. Its descendants that evolved into camels apparently migrated to Asia over the Alaskan land bridge (by which the first humans came to America in the opposite direction).

The two-humped camel has much more hair than the one-humped variety, enabling it to live in cooler climates. Its normal body temperature doesn't fluctuate as widely as its desert-dwelling cousin's. The volume of its two humps combined is about the same as the dromedary's single hump, but a single hump exposes less surface area and thus absorbs less heat. The skin over the dromedary's single hump is elastic, and expands or contracts with the size of the hump, but when the Bactrian camel loses body fat, its humps flop over.

Once, the two-humped Bactrian camel was economically important as far west as Turkey and as far south as India, but now it's found mainly in Central Asia (Uzbekistan, Tajikistan, Kirghiz, northern Afghanistan).

It's not known whether the one-humped camel evolved from the two-humped variety, but they can be crossbred, and the offspring (unlike some other hybrids, such as mules) can themselves have offspring. A cross between the two types of camels produces an animal having a long hump with a two- to five-inch depression in the middle. The child of a hybrid and a one- or two-humped camel has the same number of humps as the non-hybrid parent. In the Kirghiz language, there are many different words for the offspring of different combinations of dromedaries, Bactrians, and hybrids, down to the third generation.

Bareback camel riders usually sit *behind* the hump, but what would it feel like to sit *on* it? Author Richard W. Bulliet writes: "A camel's hump is not exactly soft and squishy, but it is nonetheless a structurally unsupported mound of fat which is subject to deformation if a heavy weight is put on top of it."

Do Headhunters and Headshrinkers Really Exist?

***

Many civilizations all over the world, from the distant past to modern times, have hunted human heads. Some of them would preserve their trophies by shrinking them. A shrunken head does not include the skull bones; it's just the skin, which has shrunk in the process of being treated and preserved.

Why would such a seemingly bizarre practice be so widespread? Many societies throughout history have regarded the head as the bodily location of consciousness, of personality, and

of the spirit. Moreover, says anthropologist Weston LaBarre, many peoples considered the head to be the source of the male fertilizing principle, because of a confused but common belief that the brain is the source of semen.

If the human spirit is located in the head, then possession of an enemy's head enabled you to use his strength and power to your own purposes—even to make him your slave in the afterlife. This belief was shared by peoples as diverse as Celtic tribes who decapitated Roman soldiers and put their heads on pikes to strengthen the Celts' forts, and some civilizations in Assam, India, in more recent times.

Drinking from a bowl made from the top of someone's skull was another way to turn the dead man's power to your own purposes, according to beliefs of some Tibetans, Bengalis, and Europeans as late as the ninth century. The traditional Scandinavian toast, *skoal,* literally means skull, and the Sanskrit word *kapāla* means both cup and skull. (But we don't think the term *mug shot* for a picture of a criminal's head is at all related!)

Severed and shrunken heads have also been important parts of fertility rites, both agricultural and human. For example, in one pre-Columbian Central American ritual, a woman dressed as the corn goddess would be decapitated, and her head would be used in a dance to ensure a good crop. Holding a severed head between the thighs has been used both as a cure for female infertility and as a manhood-initiation rite by various Australasian peoples.

Whether or not headhunting actually improved anyone's fertility, many anthropologists argue that the suppression of headhunting by colonial powers in the twentieth century did lead to the decline of many Pacific island cultures, though not for any magical or supernatural reasons. Some of these societies believed that there is a limited, fixed amount of the male lifegiving principle in the world, and that a group must constantly replenish its supply by headhunting. Women in these cultures were reluctant to marry men who hadn't successfully hunted a head, and the birth rate fell off.

This is all very interesting, we're sure, but what you *really* want to know is how to shrink a head. One of the best-documented methods is that used by the Jívaro of Amazonian Ecuador as recently as 1957, when anthropologist Michael J. Harner visited them. (He says he was even invited to join a headhunting party, but declined.) The procedure is essentially the same as that depicted in Aztec drawings over six hundred years ago, in which the Opossum God is performing a ritual with the head of an opponent who looks remarkably like Bart Simpson.

A Jívaro headhunting expedition would set off to get some "dried fish," their euphemism for shrunken heads of the neighboring Achuara people, who eat a lot of fish. After murdering a few Achuara and cutting off their heads and some flaps of chest and shoulder skin as carefully as time and pursuers permitted, the Jívaro raiders would retreat to a safe place along a river. There, they made an incision up the back of the head and peeled the skin off the skull, dropping the latter into the river as an offering to the Anaconda God. Boiling the skin in plain water ("There are no 'secret' vegetal additives," Harner advises) shrank it to about half its original size. After scraping off any remaining meat from the inside, the Jívaro sewed the skin together into its original shape, using string made from palm bark.

To shrink the head to its eventual size of somewhat bigger than a fist, the headhunters put some heated stones into the head (through the neck) and rolled them around. As the skin contracted, they switched to heated pebbles and then to sand. "Periodically, the head-taker massages the skin to help the drying process and to affect the shape," Harper explains. This activity was repeated every few hours during the party's homeward journey of about a week, and the outside of the skin was rubbed with charcoal to prevent the victim's *muisak* (avenging soul) inside the head from seeing his attackers.

On the warriors' return home, there were celebrations (most of them at the expedition leader's expense). Although there were religious aspects to the headhunting and celebrating, the primary goal was social prestige: The commander wanted to be seen both as a courageous warrior and as a generous host.

Although some anthropologists try to see "some good" in any practice of any society, even headhunting, their colleague LaBarre will have nothing of it. He lets fly at apologists who contend that headhunting benefited some civilizations by relieving boredom and by unifying the society. "Unifying . . . to what end?" he asks. "Better headhunting?"

* * *

What Does the "School Dream" or "Exam Dream" Mean?

* * *

You're in a panic, sweating, heart racing, stomach churning. You just remembered that you're scheduled to take the final examination in Something-ology 101 today, and you haven't been to class or read the textbook all semester. You don't even know where the exam is to be held.

And then you wake up.

If you frequently have the "school dream," you're not alone. In fact, you're in pretty good company. Dr. Sigmund Freud himself had a recurring dream like this, and several of the early psychoanalysts investigated it in themselves and their patients.

Freud's dream examination for which he was always unprepared was in history. "Oh," you may say, "that makes sense; he was a brilliant doctor, but he probably didn't do well in the nonscientific subjects in school." Not so. Freud said that he had "done brilliantly" in history, although he did in fact flunk an exam in forensic medicine. His contemporary, Dr. Wilhelm Stekel, stated that every one of his patients who had the school dream reported being fearful about an exam in a subject that he had passed in real life.

This meant, Freud surmised, that the school dream is often a kind of "consolation." On the eve of some "responsible activity" you're worried about—whether a job interview or an anticipated sexual encounter—the school dream tells you, "Just think how anxious you were before your exam, and yet nothing happened to you." Freud thought this interpretation applied especially to dreams in which you complain to the teacher, "I shouldn't have to take this exam. I passed it years ago, and I'm already a doctor [or whatever]!"

Such a dream might also occur, though, when the dreamer sees himself as having failed or done something wrong. In the dream you might say, "I've already passed my exams; I'm a responsible adult," but the dream's unspoken reply to that is, "Indeed you are—so you should be punished for your recent failure or transgression."

Sometimes the subject matter of the exam leads to specific analyses of a school dream. Emil A. Gutheil (a great name for a doctor—it means "good-heal" in German) wrote of one patient who dreamed of an examination in Church Law, a subject about which the patient knew nothing, and took this to represent general guilt feelings expressed as a concern about the Last Judgment, "the 'final' examination . . . before the Highest

Examiner.'' In another case, Gutheil described an impotent man's dream of worrying about an exam in *physics*.

The school dream is such a powerful symbol of danger that it can even pop up in response to a stimulus such as an uncomfortable sleeping position. Gutheil told of a patient whose real problem was that he was lying on his arm and cutting off blood circulation, but his sleeping brain turned the discomfort into a dream of anxiety and possible failure in an examination.

If you've had the school dream for a few years after you graduate from high school or college, you may think it will eventually go away. Don't get your hopes up. Even retired people who haven't seen the inside of a classroom for decades report having the dream frequently.

* * *

Who Are
Aunt Jemima
and
Uncle Ben?

* * *

The advertising trademarks Aunt Jemima *and* Uncle Ben *have sold* hundreds of millions of dollars' worth of pancakes, syrup, and rice over the past hundred years, and have prompted quite a bit of controversy over the images of African Americans used in advertising. Are they purely fictional characters, or are they based on real people? The answer is: a little bit of both.

The two characters are often linked in the public imagination, as if they were married to each other. In fact, though, the trademarks are not connected: The lady shills for the Quaker

Oats Company, while the gentleman pitches the products of Uncle Ben's, Inc.

The story begins in 1889 in St. Joseph, Missouri. The owners of a flour mill, who had just invented the first ready-made pancake mix, went to see a minstrel show. One of the acts included a popular song of the time entitled "Old Aunt Jemima," inspiring the entrepreneurs to adopt the character as the symbol for their new product. (*Aunt* and *Uncle,* of course, were titles many white Americans used condescendingly when addressing older black people.)

At first, packages of the pancake mix carried a picture from the minstrel troupe's advertising posters, which has been described as "hideous" and "poorly drawn." In 1890, though, the trademark was changed to depict the face of Nancy Green. Born into slavery in 1834, Green was hired to play the role of Aunt Jemima in a traveling ad campaign. With her picture on the box, she became the first living person to be turned into a trademark.

The pancake-mix business, though, didn't prosper. At the brink of bankruptcy, the owners staked everything on one last chance. They rented a booth at the Chicago world's fair of 1893 where Nancy Green, as Aunt Jemima, sang songs and told stories of the Old South while cooking up pancakes for her audience. She was a phenomenal hit, put the company back in the black, and became a national celebrity, touring the country touting Aunt Jemima products for the next thirty years.

Starting in 1895, little girls could send in a boxtop and a quarter for an Aunt Jemima rag doll. The toy became one of the most popular in the country, and planted the trademark in the minds of the next generation of consumers. All the advertising had been successful among the mothers of these children, too: A 1900 survey of American housewives found that Aunt Jemima was among their most trusted symbols.

Another actress, three-hundred-fifty-pound Anna Robinson, was hired to impersonate Aunt Jemima in 1933. Like Nancy Green, she became nationally famous. Edith Wilson followed her from 1948 to 1966, appearing on television as well as at in-person promotions. During each woman's tenure, it was her picture that appeared on the labels of Aunt Jemima products. At the same time, yet another live Aunt Jemima (played by Aylene Lewis) was installed at Disneyland, serving up pancakes to countless tourists, including Prime Minister Jawaharlal Nehru of India.

Meanwhile, the public relations army at Quaker Oats had been busy on another front. They invented a "historical" Aunt Jemima, who had been the cook for a Colonel Higbee in the Old South, somewhere near the Mississippi River. The "real" Jemima was credited with all sorts of improbable wonders, such as saving the passengers on a sinking steamboat by making pancake life preservers. She also used her culinary skills to distract a band of Yankee soldiers who were intent on ripping out the good colonel's impressive moustache by its roots.

By the time the last live Aunt Jemima retired in 1966, the Civil Rights movement was at flood tide. Along with major victories such as the passage of the Voting Rights Act and the desegregation of public facilities, the movement generated many smaller changes, one of which was a complete makeover of Aunt Jemima.

For almost eighty years, America's most familiar symbol of the African-American woman had been the kindly but overweight, servile, and not particularly bright Aunt Jemima, states Texas A&M journalism professor Marilyn Kern-Foxworth. The trademark was that well known, that entrenched, that powerful. Not only did the stereotype of the "mammy" distort and poison the image of black women among people of all races, Kern-Foxworth argues; it also warped the thinking of advertisers so badly that it kept them from successfully appealing to the untapped but potentially lucrative market of modern African-American female consumers.

Money talks, though, and it eventually got through to the P.R. guys that the old Aunt Jemima stereotype was not only insulting; it was bad for business. In 1968, Aunt Jemima lost about one hundred pounds and became forty years younger overnight, and tasteless ad copy phrased in white writers' mangled versions of black dialect disappeared. Aunt Jemima still wore the old-fashioned bandana, but lost it (and gained pearl earrings and a lace collar) in another makeover in 1989. *The New York Times* described Aunt Jemima's latest incarnation as looking more like the mistress of the house than like the cook.

Uncle Ben hasn't been around nearly as long as Aunt Jemima, nor has he been the subject of so much historical and marketing research. The Uncle Ben's company publishes a brochure with a story that sounds almost as fanciful as Quaker's tales of Aunt Jemima down on the old plantation. You be the judge; here's the party line on Uncle Ben:

> Many years ago, a Texas rice grower established a standard of quality that has been painstakingly preserved by Uncle Ben's, Inc.
>
> The original Uncle Ben was a Black rice farmer known to rice millers in and around Houston for consistently delivering the highest quality rice for milling. It was said that Uncle Ben harvested his rice with such care that he repeatedly received honors for full kernel yields and quality. Word has it that other rice growers proudly compared their rice, claiming it was as "good as Uncle Ben's."
>
> Although the details of Uncle Ben, the quality rice farmer, are lost to history [Authors' aside: Yeah, right.], the unique rice products which preserve his name are now known worldwide as Uncle Ben's Converted Brand Rice. Uncle Ben's proudly traces its roots back to his agricultural legend.
>
> In the late 1940s, Gordon L. Harwell, the first president of Converted Rice, Inc. (the predecessor of Uncle Ben's, Inc.) and his partner

were having dinner in their favorite Chicago restaurant. They were interested in bringing to the American consumer the same high quality rice that they had been supplying exclusively to the Armed Forces during World War II. As both men discussed the marketing strategy for a quality rice in a prominent restaurant in Chicago, the connection to Uncle Ben's quality came up in their conversation. It was then that they decided to call their product Uncle Ben's Converted Brand Rice and manufacture it in the rice-growing area around Houston.

The original Uncle Ben had passed away some years earlier, but both men felt it was appropriate to recognize him as the symbol of their quality rice products. The restaurant's maitre d', one Frank Brown, had been a close friend of both men for years, and they asked him if he would pose for the portrait which was soon to appear on millions of Converted Brand Rice cartons.

* * *

When Was the Bumper Sticker Invented?

* * *

From JONES FOR MAYOR *to* TREES, PLEASE, *to* I HAVE AN HONOR STUDENT AT CITY HIGH SCHOOL (and the reply, MY KID BEAT UP YOUR HONOR STUDENT), bumper stickers are a ubiquitous channel of communication, political expression, humor, and contempt for one's fellow man. (As National Public Radio commentator John Rosenthal says, most of them can be summarized as implying "I'm a nice person and you're not.") But surprisingly, although automobiles had been around for decades, the self-adhesive paper bumper sticker wasn't introduced until the 1956 presidential campaign. The more easily removable vinyl sticker appeared in about 1972.

Even in the early days of the motorcar, though, people did decorate their Tin Lizzies with election-campaign items. By 1920, decals intended for home windows began showing up on car windshields. The first political item specifically designed for a car was a license plate attachment promoting Calvin Coolidge for President in 1924—a tie-in with the first motorized campaign swing, the "Lincoln tour" beginning at Coolidge's home in Vermont and following the Lincoln Highway to California.

Spare tires were often located on the back of the car in the 1930s, and Herbert Hoover's campaign used them as advertising space. Oilcloth tire covers with his picture were available to voters in 1932.

The year 1932 also saw the first long, thin, rectangular signs intended for use on car bumpers. But these weren't bumper *stickers;* they had to be fastened on with string or wire.

During that same election year, Democrats produced the famous car license plate containing no words, just the faces of their candidates, Franklin D. Roosevelt and John Nance Garner, with a foaming mug of beer between them—reminding voters that the Democrats had promised to repeal Prohibition. Political-ad license plates have been in use ever since then, mostly in Southern states, which don't require real license tags on both the front and back of cars.

Finally, in 1956, both major parties introduced self-adhesive bumper stickers—over fifty varieties for the presidential candidates alone. "Inexpensive but very durable, perfectly suited to an electorate on wheels, and highly visible yet conducive to the preservation of a modicum of personal anonymity, the bumper sticker quickly developed into the most significant single avenue of personal political expression,"* writes the author of a history of the "material culture" of political campaigns.

Over two hundred different bumper stickers promoted (or

* Roger A. Fischer, *Tippecanoe and Trinkets Too* (Urbana: University of Illinois Press, 1982).

attacked) candidates in the 1964 presidential race. One, produced by supporters of Barry Goldwater before President John Kennedy's death, proclaimed that BARRY WILL FLUSH THE WHITE HOUSE JOHN. Responding in kind, Democrats adorned their cars with $C_5H_4N_4O_3$ ON AU H_2O. (The first of those chemical symbols is the formula for uric acid, which is a component of human urine; the second is "gold water.")

Similarly nasty stickers appeared in the next election year, 1968. Opponents tried to link disfavored candidates to Nazism with stickers reading WALLACE, WALLACE, ÜBER ALLES, and NIXON with the x replaced by a swastika.

National campaign organizations began to put less emphasis on bumper stickers as television became a more important campaign medium. In 1976, for example, Jimmy Carter's campaign produced no bumper stickers at all until demands from campaign workers led media director Gerald Rafshoon to give in and print up two hundred thousand. (By contrast, President Gerald Ford's campaign produced one and a half million stickers that year.) Local party organizations and Political Action Committees, though, are producing more bumper stickers than ever before.

Bumper stickers advertising specific candidates or political parties are becoming rarer, according to author Keith Melden,* but those supporting mass movements on single issues, or special interests, are proliferating. This, he says, is in line with citizens' tendencies to think of themselves less as Democrats or Republicans than as pro-life, or anti-apartheid, or environmentally conscious, or just plain overtaxed.

---

* Keith Melden, *Hail to the Candidate* (Washington, D.C.: Smithsonian Institution Press, 1992).

Do Chiggers
Really Burrow Under
Your Skin and
Lay Eggs There?

Yes, they do that—and other disgusting things, too.

First of all, though, what do you mean by *chigger*? People use that word to refer to two different animals. One is an insect, sometimes called by its Caribbean name, the chigoe flea. Its scientific name, *Dermatophilus penetrans*, means "penetrating skin-lover." This reddish-brown flea "has the despicable habit of burrowing into the skin, especially between the toes and under the toenails," according to entomologists (insect scientists) C. L. Metcalf and W. P. Flint. Normally only one millimeter long, the female, when pregnant, can grow to the size of a pea before pushing her eggs out through the host's skin, where the young hatch and grow, preferably in manure. If the egg-swollen flea is not removed in time, the host's infested toe, foot, or even entire leg may have to be amputated. The chigoe flea burrows into hogs as well as humans.

The other creature that goes by the name *chigger, jigger,* or *red bug* is not an insect at all, but rather a mite—a relative of spiders and ticks. These mites are carnivorous only in the larval stage; as adults they become vegetarians. They are smaller than the chigoe flea, often so small they are invisible to the naked eye.

What chigger mites do to humans sounds like something out of a science-fiction horror movie. They bite, but unlike mosquitoes, they don't drink blood. Instead, they inject a digestive juice that liquifies flesh. The irritated cells around the edge of the affected area harden into a cylindrical *stylostome* (Greek for ''pillar-mouth''), which the chigger uses like a straw to suck out the partially digested meat.

You probably won't see or feel the chigger while it's dissolving and drinking you. The itch you feel, and the red dot you see at the location of the bite, are caused by the stylostome, not the chigger, which has probably dropped off by then. The irritation happens because human flesh is not the chigger's preferred food. Its digestive juices evolved in such a way that they're most effective on the meat of birds or reptiles, which don't itch after a chigger bite. The itch we feel is a side effect of the imperfect match between the chigger's enzymes and our flesh. (There are a few chigger species in Asia and the Pacific whose preferred host *is* the human being, and their bites *don't* cause itching.)

Irritating as they are, chiggers generally don't carry diseases.

The main exception is a species found in Japan that spreads scrub typhus. In the rest of the world, the only way you'll get an infection from a chigger bite is by scratching it with dirty fingers.

Chiggers' mouths aren't especially strong, so they tend to bite in places where the skin is soft, particularly at skin folds like the armpits or the crotch. The myth that women *attract* more chiggers than men do is false, but women suffer more bites because their skin tends to be thinner.

Another myth that's not only false but potentially dangerous is that you have to wash with kerosene, or paint over the bite with nail polish, to get rid of chiggers. Of course, by the time you feel the itch, the chigger is gone already. To get rid of chiggers that may be on you but haven't bitten yet, biologist Nina Bicknese recommends simply taking a shower or bath. To avoid them in the first place, she recommends powdered sulfur (if you can stand the smell) or mosquito repellent. And if you want to sit down in the woods to rest or have a picnic, find a sun-warmed rock: Chiggers will avoid it, because they dislike temperatures above 99 degrees Fahrenheit.

Why Don't Birds Bounce Up When They Flap Their Wings Down, and Bounce Down When They Flap Their Wings Up?

✳ ✳ ✳

Birds don't simply flap their wings up and down. They move them in complicated patterns that differ from species to species, according to Crawford H. Greenewalt, who made a detailed investigation of bird flight for the Du Pont company.

On average, a bird's wings move downward about 60 percent of the time, providing both upward lift and forward thrust. But large, heavy birds, like owls, need to generate some lift even on the upswing, or they will lose altitude. While bringing their wings back up, they tilt them so that the leading edge is higher than the trailing edge. This causes them to lose a little forward speed, but it does produce enough lift to keep them from falling.

Smaller birds, unlike owls, don't plummet immediately if they stop flapping their wings. Their ratio of surface area to weight is much higher, so they fall more slowly, just as a feather falls more slowly than a rock. But sparrows and other little birds have a different problem: drag, or loss of forward momentum. As German ornithologist Georg Rueppell describes it, the sparrow's strategy is to separate its wing feathers like venetian blinds during the upbeat. Air can flow through, reducing drag until the bird is ready for the next downstroke. Small birds may not produce any lift on the upstroke, but at least they avoid bouncing downward.

* * *

Who Invented the Boomerang, and Why?

* * *

There are several different kinds of boomerangs, most of which don't come back to the thrower, although some do. Australians—but also Eskimos, ancient Egyptians, and people in many other areas—used them as weapons for hunting and warfare, religious objects, tokens of esteem, toys, and even musical instruments.

The oldest boomerang ever found was made of mammoth's tusk twenty-three thousand years old, not from Australia, but from Poland. Researchers didn't want to risk breaking it, so they didn't throw the tusk itself, but a replica of it did return when thrown. The oldest Australian boomerang, made of wood, dates back ten thousand years, and there are rock paintings over fifteen thousand years old in Australia depicting boomerangs. The aborigines have many different words for the device, but the one that's survived in English is *bumariny,* from the Dharuk language formerly spoken near the area that's now Sydney.

The boomerang started as a refinement of a simple stick thrown as a weapon. Somebody apparently noticed that certain pieces of wood flew farther when thrown than others, and began looking for (or making) sticks in that same shape. The reason for the difference is aerodynamics. A plain old stick, when thrown horizontally, falls vertically as it travels, and eventually hits the ground, making it useless as a weapon beyond a certain distance. But a stick of the right shape can generate lift as it travels through the air, like an airplane wing, and stay aloft longer. This kind of stick may have twice the range of the standard model.

Another advantage that a whirling boomerang has over a spear is the wide swath it cuts. While a spear or rock has to be thrown right on target, a boomerang can be a foot or so wide of its mark and still deliver a blow to its victim. Moreover, the rotating motion gives the leading edge more momentum than the mere forward motion of other missiles.

You had to know your boomerang, though. Because they weren't mass-produced, and because their users weren't aware of the aerodynamic principles and formulas behind boomerang flight, each boomerang had its own personality, its own flight pattern. You had to be familiar with just how it would travel before you could throw it with accuracy.

Necessity being the mother of invention, people on the receiving end of boomerang warfare came up with defensive measures. One such idea was the Australian woomera, a stick with a hook on the end that could knock or grab a boomerang out of the air.

Military technology, however, never stands still: The response was the "number 7" boomerang. The weapon is shaped like the digit 7, or like a regular boomerang with a little hook on one end. The hook allows the "number 7" to hang on to a defender's woomera or shield, whip around, and conk him on the back of the head.

Old boomerangs have been found in parts of Australia where the local people never made them, and never used them as weapons or toys. They seem to have traveled as gifts from tribes farther south. The recipients sometimes used them as "clapsticks" to make music.

In other parts of the world, the invention of the bow and arrow apparently put boomerang makers out of business, but Australians continued to use their traditional weapon, not only for warfare, but also to hunt game, and even to stun big fish swimming in shallow tidal pools.

Returning boomerangs, probably the most famous kind, have been found all over the world, but in Australia, they were limited to the eastern part of the continent. The aborigines used them for throwing practice while training to use the one-way version, and also for sports. One game was similar to the American schoolchildren's pastime of "dodgeball," though the use of a hardwood boomerang probably gave the Australian players more of an incentive to avoid being hit! Another sport involved throwing the boomerang at a stick in the ground—a bit like modern-day horseshoes, except that you can't throw a horseshoe past the stake and have it circle back for a ringer.

The returning boomerang was traditionally made from the wood at the joint between a tree's trunk and root. The optimal angle of the bend is 109 degrees. A typical boomerang has a wingspan of one or two feet, and weighs from one to six ounces. Like an airplane wing, it has one convex side and one that's more or less flat. The shape of the finished product is almost like a three-bladed propeller with one blade missing. Each of the two halves has its own name: the *lifting* (leading) arm and the *dingle* (trailing) arm. (In the rain forests of Australia's extreme northeast, there were also four-bladed, X-shaped returning boomerangs.)

To make a boomerang come back, the thrower tosses it into the wind, in an almost vertical plane. (By contrast, the one-way boomerang, used as a weapon, was tossed horizontally, like a flying disc, so as to whack as many of the enemy or prey as possible.) Complex interactions of aerodynamic forces and the gyroscope-like behavior of the rotating blade combine to cause the boomerang to travel in a loop and end up where it started, or to trace a figure *8* or more complicated pattern.

Today, aficionados of boomerang sport get together to compete even in countries far from the land down under. There's a U.S. Boomerang Association (USBA) and there are two newsletters—*The Leading Edge* and *Many Happy Returns.* Events include accuracy (*you* are the bullseye), trick catching, maximum time aloft (world's record: almost three minutes), and juggling (world's record: over three hundred fifty catches in a row). And judging from the letter we got from Chet Snouffer of the USBA, if you want to be cool, you have to call the thing a *boom,* though *rang* is apparently acceptable, too.

* * *

Why Do Audiences *Boo* When They Don't Like the Performance?

* * *

*I*n the birthplace of European theater, Athens of the fifth and fourth centuries B.C., the authorities tried to keep audience reaction to plays from getting out of hand. After all, the annual theater festival was a religious observance in honor of the god Dionysus. Violence in the audience was punishable by death, and playwrights were discouraged from presenting anything that would get the audience too worked up. Consequently, although there are plenty of murders in Greek tragedies, they all take place offstage.

But the festival was also a competition among playwrights, and audiences did make their preferences known. According to theater historian Jacques Burdick, "They applauded loudly what they admired, but they stamped, shouted, and whistled when they found the presentation inferior." And an unconfirmed but traditional story has it that the audience once hissed and threatened Aeschylus so viciously that the great tragedian had to climb onto the holy altar of Dionysus for sanctuary.

A few hundred years later, in imperial Rome, audiences continued to voice approval or disdain. Actors played to a "noisy, jostly crowd in holiday mood which was just as liable to boo actors who failed to arrest and maintain their attention as to applaud those who amused them," writes theater historian Glynne Wickham. Authors and actors, who stood to get cash bonuses if their work was well received, sometimes bribed audience members to react approvingly.

Both ancient Greek and Latin had words sounding like the English word *boh,* all of which mean "to shout." The *Oxford English Dictionary* speculates that these words occur because the sound *bo* or *boo* is "a combination of consonant and vowel especially fitted to produce a loud and startling sound." And loud and startling is exactly what an unhappy audience wants to be.

Audiences have been known to boo the theater management as well as the actors. When the Roman emperor Tiberius banished some popular actors because of their blatantly immoral behavior, theater fans raised such a ruckus that he had to let the actors return. In England, a few decades after Shakespeare's time, actors sometimes went on stage and complained to the audiences about their pay, inciting the public to riot if the theater management didn't give in to their salary demands.

The custom of throwing rotten fruit at bad actors doesn't seem to be quite as old as booing. But it does date back at least four hundred years: Spanish audiences of that time brought along not only putrid produce, but also whistles and noisemakers to use in case they didn't like the performance.

* * *

Why Do We Cross Our Fingers to Mean "Good Luck" or "I'm Lying"?

* * *

The gesture of the crossed middle and index fingers has two very different meanings, but they may both come from the same source. Nobody has a definitive answer, but animal-behavior expert Desmond Morris, who has investigated this and other familiar gestures, has some theories.

"Although there is very little evidence to go on," Morris writes,* he would "tend to accept" the explanation that the

---

* Desmond Morris, *Gestures: Their Origin and Distribution* (London: Jonathan Cape, 1979).

gesture is a stylized sign of the cross. When people wish you good luck by crossing their fingers, it's symbolic that they're praying for you or invoking God's good graces. When someone tells a fib, it's an attempt to ward off punishment for the sin of lying.

Children in England and elsewhere also use crossed fingers as a sign of "protection," holding the gesture out against other children much as one would hold up a cross or a garlic pod against a vampire. Morris speculates that this, too, can be traced back to the sign of the cross.

Morris mentions some other possible explanations for the gesture. The pope's method of blessing—a hand held up with the index and middle fingers pointing upward and crossed—could explain the association of crossed fingers with wishes of good luck. In this sign, the middle (longest) finger, crossed in front of the other, is supposed to represent Christ victorious over evil. The use of the gesture to excuse a lie, on the other hand, could come from an association between crossing fingers and crossing out something that has been written—the lie is crossed out or negated.

Crossed fingers have other meanings as well. Some ancient Romans believed that the gesture could prevent pregnancy. (We think it would be more effective to cross the legs.) In some Middle Eastern cultures, the sign represents friendship; if you're very angry with someone, you make the sign, but then violently separate the fingers with a finger of the other hand, to signify the breaking of the friendship.

* * *

How Did
the Question Mark
Get Its Shape?

* * *

The question mark, and other punctuation symbols, exist because Saint Augustine and Charlemagne wanted to save your soul. But we're getting ahead of the game. First, a little ancient history.

Long ago, Western and Middle Eastern languages didn't have any punctuation at all, except for the Babylonians and Assyrians, who put a space at the end of each sentence. Words ran into each other with no indication of where one began and another ended. The Persians began putting signs such as "<"

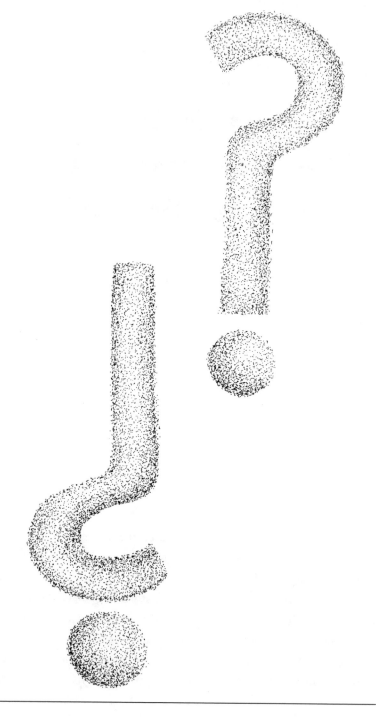

or ":" between words in about the seventh century B.C., but the practice of separating words didn't catch on in European languages until hundreds of years later.

A Roman who could read a text at first sight was considered a marvel; most literate people had to spend a good deal of time just grouping the string of letters on the page into meaningful words. Sometimes a text could mean different things, depending on where the reader separated the words. Virgil's *Aeneid*, for instance, contains the sequence CONSPICITVRSVS, which can be read *conspicit ursus* (the bear sees) or *conspicitur sus* (the pig is seen), and the letters EXILIO, which could be either *ex Ilio* (from Troy) or *exilio* (in exile).

Beginning in about the second century B.C., some Greek and Latin manuscripts, especially those used for educational purposes, had dots between the words. In some cases, they even had rudimentary punctuation, to help the student of oratory learn where to pause when speaking. In one system, a dot below the line was equivalent to today's comma, one in the middle of the line was like a colon or semicolon, and one above the line meant a full stop.

Punctuation didn't really catch on until about A.D. 600, when it had become a matter of eternal life and death. Most people in the Western world were illiterate, so their only contact with the Bible and other religious literature occurred when a priest read out loud from the pulpit. Saint Augustine, the fifth-century African bishop and author, warned that if the priest paused in the wrong place while reading, it could change the meaning of the words, thus misleading the people into an incorrect interpretation of the Word of God and causing their eternal damnation. Bummer!

To make sure that clerics read the holy texts correctly, scholars and copyists inserted various dots and squiggles into manuscripts. Often, they used the same symbol for the end of a statement and the end of a question, because in Latin, the word order and other grammatical clues made it easy to tell the difference without the aid of punctuation.

In the ninth century, the court of Charlemagne adopted a fixed set of punctuation marks that soon became the standard throughout Europe. These included a sign for the end of an interrogatory sentence that looks somewhat like today's question mark: a dot with a backward-*S* squiggle above and to the right of it. Sometimes this was represented as an upside-down semicolon, or a dot with a tilde ($\tilde{\cdot}$) directly over it, but it's easy to see how such a symbol could evolve into ?.

Within a century of the introduction of the printing press in Europe, most punctuation symbols had taken on their modern-day shapes. In the Gutenberg Bibles of the mid-fifteenth century, the upper hooked part of the question mark is what we'd consider upside down, with the straight line extending upward, instead of downward toward the dot, like this: [⸮]. By the 1500s, the right-side-up version (?) had become the standard. It was very expensive to create a completely new typeface, so as the printing press spread, so did copies of the existing type fonts of letters, numbers, and punctuation.

Since then, there have been a few other developments in question-mark technology. One printer, around 1580, used a backward question mark to indicate a rhetorical question, and a regular one for questions that required an answer, but this didn't catch on. In about 1750, the Spanish Royal Academy decreed that sentences ending in a question mark should begin with an inverted question mark, so readers wouldn't have to glance ahead to the end of the sentence to find out whether it was a question. The Spanish-speaking world still uses this convention today.

The Spanish do the same thing with the exclamation point,

which is a latecomer to the world of punctuation, first appearing in the 1300s. One theory of its origin is that scribes would indicate an exclamatory *Oh!* by writing an *O* with an accent mark above it. From there it's a small step to the modern exclamation point!

* * *

How Do Peking, Szechuan, and Cantonese Food Differ?

* * *

Gourmets recognize dozens of different schools of Chinese cooking. But don't panic. There are four main categories of Chinese food, and they're easy to learn and distinguish: the Northern, Eastern, Western, and Southern styles.

Northern Chinese cuisine includes the cookery of the capital city, Beijing, formerly known as Peking. Because wheat, not rice, is the staple grain grown in that region, many dishes are based on noodles (for example, lo mein) and pancakes or crepes (like Peking duck). Sauces are generally mild, and frequently sweet, like the hoisin sauce served with Peking duck. Northern coastal areas make sweet-and-sour fish stews. Lamb is a favorite meat in the North, thanks to the culinary influence of nearby Mongolia, but it isn't especially popular in the rest of China.

The North's growing season is shorter than that of other regions, so Northern cooks use ingredients that keep well throughout the winter. Typical items include onions, cabbage, smoked meat, and preserved vegetables (including "monkey's head," which is a kind of dried mushroom).

Eastern Chinese cooking comes from the areas around Shanghai and Nanking. To foreigners, this is probably the least well-known style of Chinese food. Instead of quick stir-frying, many Eastern recipes call for slow simmering. The Eastern province of Fukien is famous for its rich soy sauce, which gives color and flavor to so-called red-cooked stews.

Because of the long coastline and great rivers in Eastern China, seafood is plentiful. Sauces contain lots of sugar and oil, "giving this area a reputation for rich food," according to television's Chinese chef Ken Hom.

Bird's-nest soup is a delicacy of Eastern Chinese cuisine. It really does contain a bird's nest, but not just any bird's nest. The soup is made by boiling the nest of the swiftlet, a cave-dwelling bird whose nest is made largely of "concentric layers of . . . a mucilaginous secretion of the salivary gland," according to the *Encyclopaedia Brittanica*. "The substance, rich in protein, is clear, whitish, and brittle before it is boiled." The more of this goo a nest contains, and the fewer twigs and other pieces of plant matter, the higher the price of the nest.

The hot and spicy cooking of Hunan and Szechuan provinces are familiar examples of Western Chinese food. Peppers of all sorts, ginger, and garlic, give strong flavor to this region's dishes. Sometimes sweet or sour flavors are combined with the heat. "Tree ear" mushrooms are also a trademark of Western Chinese cuisine.

Southern (Cantonese) cuisine was the first Chinese food with which many Occidentals became familiar, because the first wave of Chinese immigration to Europe and the Americas was largely from that area. Rice is the staple grain in Canton city and surrounding Kwangtung province, and is served along with such well-known Cantonese dishes as egg rolls, moo goo gai pan, and egg foo young.

The food is typically light, fresh, and only lightly spiced. For example, "blanched chicken" consists simply of boiled chicken, sliced and served with a variety of sauces to dip it in.

Like other coastal areas, Southern China uses seafood in many dishes. Shrimp dumplings, for example, are a popular item in restaurants that serve "dim sum"—an infinite variety of steamed and fried dumplings and other appetizers. A Hong Kong tradition, dim sum is also becoming popular outside China. Waiters constantly pass by diners' tables, wheeling carts loaded with small plates or bamboo steamers, each of which contains a few pieces of one type of dim sum. Customers pick up whatever looks good to them from the cart.

Chow mein (stir-fried noodles) is a Southern Chinese dish, but another favorite on Chinese-restaurant menus in America, chop suey, didn't come from China at all. According to one story, told by cookbook author Emily Hahn, chop suey was born when a Chinese diplomat abroad, suffering from an upset stomach, asked his cook to whip up something as bland and boring as possible. Another story attributes chop suey to the attempts of Chinese railroad workers in the American West to cook up something they'd like better than American food. The name comes from the Cantonese *shap sui,* literally "miscellaneous bits."

A final word on Southern Chinese cuisine comes from an encyclopedia published by the Chinese Academy of Social Sciences. Its list of typical Cantonese dishes includes snake meat, and a stew of dog entrails. When cooking, say these experts, dog has "a strong, appetizing smell."

* * *

Where Do Sleepwalkers Walk?

* * *

*L*ots of places, and sometimes into trouble! *Sleepwalking (somnambu* lism) is one of several sleep phenomena known as parasomnias (which means "faulty sleep"). It is one of the so-called disorders of arousal involving sleep states in which the victim is caught in an intermediate state between snoozing and grooving. Sleepwalking is most common in children, with its highest incidence occurring between the ages of four and eight, and usually disappears after puberty. The behavior can be as innocuous as simply sitting up in bed, or as complex as walking out the door, getting in the car, and driving off. Sleepwalking behaviors tend to be limited to automatisms, that is, actions that we all learn to perform automatically, with little active thought. That's why driving a car, something that becomes second nature to us all, is within the capabilities of a sleepwalker. Sleepwalkers will rearrange furniture (with no logic to the result), walk out of windows, and converse, though the dialogue is unintelligible because making sense requires higher brain function. In addition to the hazards of leaving the house, driving, and clumsiness, sleepwalkers sometimes fall into a panic to "escape." Cooking has been recorded in some cases (imagine the dangers involved when a person who's technically asleep stands at the gas stove in a flammable nightgown, cooking french fries and carving a roast with a Ginsu knife!). The episodes can be triggered by external events, such as a noise, or internal stimuli, such as a full bladder (sleepwalking into an area other than the bathroom to pee is common among children). In reality, injuries are uncommon—still, the hazards remain. Two rarer forms of sleepwalking have obvious health implications: sleep-eating (repeated bouts of chowing down that may lead to weight problems) and sleep-drunkenness.

Waking a sleepwalker is difficult, and may result in an attack. Sleepwalkers rarely, if ever, remember the event. The best treatment available, if the cause (such as certain medications) is not known, is to remove dangerous objects from the bedroom, lock windows, and lock the bedroom door (provided someone else can let the sleepwalker out in an emergency!). Some patients loosely bind themselves to a bed post, but sometimes learn to undo their bonds.

Brain activity during sleep shows several distinct patterns when measured by electroencephalograph (EEG). There are two basic states: Rapid Eye Movement (REM)—which involves the implied pattern of eye activity and is the state in which we dream; and Non-Rapid Eye Movement (NREM)—which is divided into four stages. In stage-one NREM, the sleeper is in a twilight between reality and sleep and shows reduced responses to stimuli. Genuine sleep starts in stage-two NREM, and stages three and four make up what is known as slow-wave sleep. A typical sleep episode involves a rather complicated cycling between REM sleep and the NREM stages, but on average, we spend about 20 percent of the night in the dream state (REM). The ability to distinguish the various states and stages using an EEG is critical in diagnosing some sleep disorders.

But back to the parasomnias. In addition to sleepwalking, other disorders of arousal are confusional arousal and sleep terrors.

Confusional arousal is common up to the age of five, and involves a state of confusion, disorientation, and slow responses while and after awakening.

With sleep terrors, the victim awakens in a state of panic, with associated rapid heartbeat and other physiological symptoms of terror, and often initiates the whole event with a blood-curdling scream. In children, sleep terrors typically commence between ages two and ten, and disappear during puberty. This is one of the cases mentioned earlier in which an EEG can be helpful. Sleep terrors are *not* nightmares. Nightmares are dreams and therefore occur during REM sleep; sleep terrors occur during NREM sleep.

Other parasomnias that are *not* arousal disorders include hypnagogic hallucinations, sleep paralysis, sleep starts, bruxism, rhythmic movement disorder, REM behavior disorder, and last, but not least, everybody's favorite: nightmares.

If you've ever had a dream that started before you were fully asleep, and whatever was in your field of view within the room was part of the dream (or, often, the nightmare), you've likely had a hypnagogic hallucination.

Sleep paralysis involves a short period of physical paralysis following arousal, whereas "sleep starts" involve a sudden whole-body jerk just as one falls asleep.

Sleep bruxism (toothgrinding) is common (possibly found in 20 percent of the population) and produces dental problems only in severe cases.

Rhythmic movement disorder involves rocking and head banging, usually in young children during and just around the sleep cycle, and is usually neither harmful nor indicative of an underlying problem.

REM behavior disorder (RBD), on the other hand, is serious business. Normally, during REM sleep, most of the body is essentially paralyzed. With RBD, this is not the case. Victims act out their dreams, thrashing their arms and legs more or less as appropriate to the ongoing action of the dream (this has been confirmed by comparing the behavioral notes made by the bed partners of patients with the patients' descriptions of their dream sequences). Amazingly, these thrashers are rarely awakened by their physical exploits. However, injury to themselves or bed partners is common. A person displaying symptoms of RBD should seek medical treatment, as various serious neurological disorders may be the underlying cause.

There is some evidence that nightmares (or for those of you who want to use the fancy-pants term: Dream Anxiety Attacks) may be up to four times as common in women as men, though some researchers speculate that these numbers may be skewed by a tendency in men to underreport nightmares. A nightmare rate of one or more per week is considered "frequent" by somnologists.

We were curious about possible nightmare treatments, and in a letter to the American Sleep Disorders Association, we asked about one treatment in particular. In an episode of the popular television series *Star Trek: The Next Generation,* the ship's physician, Dr. Crusher, treats the ship's counselor, Deanna

Troi, with a technique designed to combat nightmares: "directed dreaming." Is this for real, we asked, or standard TV jive?

Gregory Mader of ASDA had this to say about that:

"Of note is that Dr. Crusher of the USS *Enterprise* knows her medicine. Researchers at the University of New Mexico School of Medicine have reported success in 'imagery rehearsal. . . .' Dr. Crusher gives us confidence in the future—presently an average of 1.16 hours of medical-school training are spent on the study of sleep and its disorders. If Dr. Crusher knows about imagery rehearsal, then our descendants are teaching/learning more about sleep."

In the UNM imagery-rehearsal study, nightmare sufferers were told to record their nightmares carefully, then write down modified, nonscary versions of the dreams, and rehearse them in their minds. The technique was used for both recurrent and nonrecurrent nightmares. No instructions were given as to what part of the nightmare to modify; some changed the ending, some the beginning, and some the whole dream.

For example, suppose one of the study participants dreamed he was walking toward his house, smelled smoke, turned the corner, and saw that the house was on fire. He ran to the house, but the flames were overwhelming, and he could hear the screams of agony from his wife.

A typical modified version for use in imagery rehearsal might be: He's walking toward his house, smells smoke, turns the corner, and sees that his wife has steaks on the barbecue out front. He walks up, kisses her on the cheek, sits down, and pops open a brew.

The technique was used for three months, then evaluated. The subjects showed a substantial reduction in nightmare frequency, as well as related phenomena such as anxiety and depression. Interestingly, another group of people who did not use imagery rehearsal (the control group) but did keep diaries of their nightmares also showed a substantial reduction in nightmare frequency, but changes in related phenomena were not significant. The researchers speculate that writing down nightmares may, by itself, be an effective treatment.

Two serious sleep disorders that are *not* parasomnias are narcolepsy and sleep apnea.

Narcolepsy is a condition that causes excessive sleepiness in victims during the day, to the point where their drowsiness affects their ability to function, and they fall asleep at inappropriate times (such as during a staff meeting) or even catastrophic times (while driving). Another symptom is cataplexy, in which a sudden but brief loss of muscle control occurs, varying from a minor muscle weakness to a total bodily collapse, and is often triggered by anxiety or the advent of a strong and sudden emotion, including laughter. The victim remains fully aware of his circumstances. This symptom affects 60 percent of all narcoleptics. This is a permanent disorder currently believed to have a genetic basis. One of the best therapies is to arrange for the individual to take several short naps during the day. It is a cruel irony that many narcoleptics have trouble sleeping at night!

Sleep apnea is a condition in which breathing stops at frequent intervals during sleep, with the resultant and recurrent plunge in oxygen levels in the blood having serious implications for the patient's cardiovascular system. (*Apnea* is from the Greek for "want of breath.") With central sleep apnea, the regulation of breathing is temporarily suspended, which may indicate a neurological condition. With obstructive sleep apnea (OSA), the airway becomes blocked. The sleeper struggles to breathe, and then is aroused to a minimal wake state, at which point breathing resumes with a gasp. Snoring is always indicative of at least a partial obstruction of the upper airway, and loud, continuous snoring with frequent pauses followed by gasping inhalation strongly suggests OSA. OSA is the most common apnea, occurring in 1 or 2 percent of adults (it is most common in overweight middle-aged men).

A number of factors can cause the obstruction. Excessive weight is one, and sometimes moderate weight loss cures the condition entirely. Enlarged tonsils and adenoids, as well as nasal obstructions, are causative, as is an unusually narrow throat passage. In most cases, muscles at the base of the tongue and the uvula (that little dingle-dangle of tissue at the top and center of your throat) simply relax sufficiently to close the passage.

When OSA is suspected, the patient is generally sent to a sleep disorders center for evaluation. If OSA is present, and the source of the problem is not the tonsils, adenoids, or nasal passages, then there are two common treatments.

Continuous positive airway pressure (CPAP) treatment involves sleeping with a mask over the nose that is connected to an air compressor. The compressor forces a gentle stream of air through the nose that keeps the airway unobstructed. Uvulo-palatopharyngoplasty (UPPP—and boy, are we glad we didn't become doctors!) is a surgical procedure that chops out the uvula and carves out some unnecessary tissue in the upper airway. UPPP can generate two occasional side effects: nasal speech, and nasal regurgitation (fluids reflux into the nose when swallowed). Devices to manipulate the tongue or jaw by pulling them forward have shown some promise, but are not widely used. In some patients, and indeed in some snorers who don't have actual apnea, the problem is positional—they sleep on their backs. A common cure for this (one of the authors' fathers has used this and it works!) is to sew a pocket on the back of the pajama top, around the spine, and insert one or more tennis balls in it. It prevents supine sleeping, and certainly is less disruptive than a punch in the gizzard from an angry spouse! As a last resort, a surgical hole is cut in a patient's throat (a tracheostomy), through which a tube is inserted, to aid breathing through the night. The hole is kept plugged during the day.

Some sleep disorders are potentially life threatening, and others can be confused with symptoms of much more serious underlying illness. We were surprised to learn that more people die during standard sleeping hours than at any other time of the day! Interestingly, death rates increase significantly for people who sleep fewer than four hours or more than ten per night.

The best course with any sleep problem is to seek medical treatment, and leave the rest to the doctor.

Did Medieval Husbands Really Make Their Wives Wear Chastity Belts While They Were Away on Crusades?

* * *

Probably not, but the chastity belt isn't just a common (if you'll excuse the expression) misconception, either. There *are* written and pictorial references to chastity belts in European texts going back eight hundred years, and actual specimens exist, manufactured between the year 1600 and the present day. There are accounts of lawsuits against men who abused their wives with such devices in the twentieth century. And in cultures all over the world, there have been practices designed to keep both males and females from masturbating or having illicit sex. Whether all this evidence adds up to millions of medieval damsels in distress desperately seeking locksmiths, though, is questionable at best.

The oldest reference to a chastity belt in European literature does date from the period of the crusades (which were waged from 1095 to 1270). In that particular story, the belt was made of cloth, suggesting that it may have been merely symbolic of a pledge of fidelity, not a functioning appliance. Other texts from about the same time refer to a chastity belt with a "key," although that too could be metaphorical, not literal.

The oldest known illustration of a woman wearing a chastity belt is a 1405 Italian picture. By the 1500s, German literature had stories of women who paid locksmiths (with their husbands' money) to free them from the devices. The earliest surviving specimens date from about 1600, long after the end of what we now call the medieval period or Middle Ages. One such example was found in a grave, still locked, guarding the maidenly virtue of a skeleton.

Everybody understands the general principle of the chastity belt, but if you think about the details, you begin to realize that a working model would require some fancy engineering. The section of the human body between the waist and the thighs is involved in a lot more physical functions than the one the chastity belt is intended to restrict. All chastity belts had some kind of openings in the front—little holes like a colander, or a thin slit, or a larger oval-shaped opening fringed with sharp pointed "teeth." Many belts also included a metal strip guarding the rear, often with an unpleasantly impractical-looking trefoil-shaped hole supposedly to permit defecation. The *belt* part of the chastity belt—the part that went around the waist— was usually made of flexible metal, but the business end was not necessarily metal as well, but was sometimes a contoured piece of carved bone or ivory.

There seems to be no doubt that *some* men did make their wives wear the "girdle of chastity," though not necessarily in the Middle Ages, and not necessarily in large numbers. Danish law books record a case from the island of Falster, in about 1650, in which a woman took her husband to court for making her wear a chastity belt. This is evidence that such devices really were used. But the fact that the man was found guilty and banished suggests that, far from being common, the practice of making one's wife wear a chastity belt was considered as weird and as criminal in seventeenth-century Denmark as it would be here and now. And there has been a smattering of similar cases reported in various European countries in the years since.

There are stories of a chastity-belt trial in France a hundred years before the Danish case, but it's not not clear whether it was a real lawsuit, or one of the playful *Causes Grasses,* burlesque law cases that were part of Mardi Gras revelry.

Much of our present-day knowledge about chastity belts would not be possible had it not been for the exertions of a unique historian, Eric John Dingwall, who apparently spent a good portion of the years between the World Wars traveling around Europe researching the subject. He published *Male Infibulation* (the title alone is enough to make men cross their legs tightly) in 1925, and his magnum opus, *The Girdle of Chastity,* in 1931.

The history of chastity belts may not have begun in the Middle Ages, as is commonly believed, but it didn't end with the coming of modern times, either. In the last couple of centuries, chastity-beltlike garments have been promoted by various cranks, quacks, and weirdos as means of preventing youngsters from playing with themselves. There's a record of such a device in Germany in 1781; and in 1842, Scottish "doctor" John Moodie (at least he *claimed* to be a doctor) seems to have caused quite a stir by recommending chastity belts in a book entitled *A Medical Treatise: With Principles and Observations to Preserve Chastity and Morality.*

Entrepreneurs have continued to hawk chastity belts for their supposed original purpose, too. About a hundred years ago, a Monsieur Cambon of Cassagnes-Comtaux, France, offered chastity belts made by a surgical-instrument firm at prices from 120 to 320 francs. His advertisements exploited men's fear of infidelity and doubts about the paternity of their children. In 1903, a Berliner, Emilie Schäfer, applied for and received a patent on her version of the chastity belt. Today, purveyors of sex toys sell the devices to fetishists.

The most audacious chastity-belt capitalists of modern times must be the firm in Dorset, England, that applied for a tax exemption in 1969, wanting to take advantage of a loophole providing tax breaks to manufacturers of—safety equipment!

Do Elephants Breathe Through Their Trunks?

Yes, they do. An elephant's trunk is divided along its entire length into two nostrils. Not only can the elephant breathe through the trunk, it can also sneeze—an action generating so much force that it "can stun a dog," according to Heathcote Williams, author of the book *Sacred Elephant.*

In addition to regular breathing and occasional sneezing, an elephant can use its trunk as a communications device. By blowing air out while slapping the trunk against the ground, the elephant makes a sound similar to sheet metal being shaken, which is thought to indicate dislike or fear. Elephants greet each other with a squeaky sound from their trunks. And of course, there's the well-known "trumpeting" sound, heard on the soundtrack of every Tarzan movie. The word *trunk* itself is due to its musical qualities; the name is derived from the French *trompe,* meaning *trumpet.* (And while we're on word origins, *pachyderm,* another term for elephant, is Greek for "thick skin.")

Having a schnoz even longer than Jimmy Durante's—eight feet long in a grown elephant—enables the elephant to cross deep rivers and lakes, using its trunk as a snorkel. Even on dry land, the trunk can act as a snorkel, or a periscope, by picking up airborne smells from above the tops of the surrounding

vegetation. This helps compensate for the elephant's poor eyesight.

Elephants also use the sense of smell to recognize each other. They frequently touch their trunks together or intertwine them as a greeting, and have been known to spend up to three days in a kind of pachyderm foreplay, stroking and smelling each other's musth glands (located on the cheeks).

The list of things elephants can do with their trunk, used as a nose, is impressive, but that's only the beginning of all they can do with this marvelous limb. Or, to be more accurate, lip: The trunk is an elongated combination of the nose and upper lip. The ancient Aryan people of northern India called it the elephant's "head finger," and in addition to looking like a huge finger, the trunk ends in one or two small, sensitive, dextrous fingers. (The Indian elephant has one finger, the African has two.) With these fingers the animal can perform such precise tasks as pulling a thorn out of its foot or drawing pictures and words with a piece of chalk.

The sixty thousand trunk muscles can be used to perform not only delicate manipulations, but also great feats of strength. An elephant can shake a tree to dislodge fruit that's too high for it to reach, or even pull it up by its roots. An attacking animal may find itself picked up and tossed into the air or even crushed against the elephant's broad forehead.

Mother elephants can pick up their young, called *calves*, and carry them. An adult—not always the calf's mother, but usually a female—may quieten or discipline an annoying calf by slapping or shoving it with her trunk.

The trunk is useful in getting water to drink, but the elephant doesn't actually drink *through* the trunk. It sucks water into its trunk and then squirts it into its mouth. (Baby elephants don't use their trunks to suckle, though; just their mouths.) To get to a water table just below the surface of the ground, an elephant can use its tusks and trunk as pick and shovel to dig a hole.

To keep cool, elephants sometimes fill their trunks with water and spray it on themselves or others. The great exposed surface area of the trunk also helps the animal to regulate its temperature by radiating heat, as do its huge ears (which it can also flap to create a breeze).

It takes a lot of energy to carry a three-hundred-pound trunk around on your head all the time, so the elephant sometimes takes a load off by draping its trunk over a tusk. Despite the heavy burden, though, the elephant can't afford to be without its trunk; it wouldn't be able to eat. Unlike a horse, an elephant, with its short, thick neck, can't bend its head to the ground to eat, so it has to have the trunk to carry food to its mouth.

* * *

Does the Catholic Church Still Perform Exorcisms?

* * *

Exorcism is a part of many cultures, often serving a purpose similar to that of psychotherapy in Western societies. The term comes from Greek words meaning *out* and *oath*. Roman Catholics are still among the practitioners of exorcism. In 1990, for example, New York Archbishop John J. O'Connor announced that two "successful" exorcisms had recently taken place in his archdiocese.

The archbishop said that cases of diabolical possession are

"very rare." Depending on how you define exorcism, though, the practice itself is not rare at all, in the Catholic church or elsewhere. Several Catholic ceremonies, including baptism and the blessing of holy water, contain exorcisms. (In a chapter entitled "Memories of a Catholic Boyhood,"* author Garry Wills recalled "baptisms in the spittle of repeated *Exorcizo's*"— the Latin word for *I exorcise,* which, when pronounced with an Italian *c* and *z,* does indeed cause a lot of spray.) This kind of exorcism is not intended to cast out evil spirits, but to protect the person or object from Satan and Co. As the *New Catholic Encyclopedia* says offhandedly, "exorcism is nothing more than a prayer to God . . . to restrain the power of the demon over men and things."†

Nevertheless, the Catholic church does still exorcise people who it contends are possessed by devils. The rite is performed only with permission of the local bishop, and only after many less drastic steps, such as medical and psychological examinations and treatment, have failed. According to another source: "Elements of the rite include the Litany of Saints [a prayer asking the intercession of dozens of individually named saints]; recitation of the *Our Father,* one or more creeds, and other prayers; specific prayers of exorcism; the reading of Gospel passages, and use of the Sign of the Cross."‡

Catholic exorcism is not a major sacrament (such as baptism, marriage, or the last blessing of the dying), but rather, a "sacramental," defined as a "sacred sign [that] signifies effects, particularly of a spiritual kind, which are obtained through the Church's intercession."§ Examples of sacramentals other than exorcism include holy water, saints' medals and candles, and

---

* *Bare Ruined Choirs* (Garden City, N.Y.: Doubleday, 1972).
† *New Catholic Encyclopedia* (New York: McGraw-Hill, 1967).
‡ *1993 Catholic Almanac* (Huntington, Ind.: Our Sunday Visitor, Inc., 1993).
§ Ibid.

blessings, ranging from the 1990 blessing (not exorcism) of an Indiana house in which the presence of a teenage Satanist was said to be making objects fly about of their own accord, to the specific formula laid down in the *Roman Ritual* for the dedication of a seismograph.

Since the third century, the office of exorcist was one of the church's minor orders (a category including such positions as acolyte and reader, as distinguished from major orders such as the diaconate and the priesthood). Along with the office of porter, it was abolished in 1973, which coincidentally was the year Linda Blair entertained movie audiences by spewing green bile all over Max von Sydow in *The Exorcist*.

Some Protestant churches also recognize exorcism. Missionaries living among peoples whose traditional beliefs include possession sometimes ingratiate themselves with the locals by exorcising evil spirits. The Episcopal church recognizes exorcism, at least on paper, but it doesn't prescribe a specific ritual. Buried deep in the *Book of Occasional Services* (a companion to the *Book of Common Prayer* but much less well known) is a statement that anyone who is "in need of such a ministry" should ask his parish priest to contact the bishop, who will decide whether and how the exorcism is to take place.

Some Japanese Buddhist sects have been performing exorcisms for at least a thousand years. The eleventh-century *Tale of Genji* describes exorcisms carried out by Buddhist priests assisted by young girls and adult women as mediums. Modern-day Japanese exorcists train by living on cold mountaintops for weeks, forgoing sleep and food, and subjecting themselves to other deprivations. They cast out demons, animal spirits, or the neglected ghosts of deceased humans by talking to the possessed person, chanting from the *Lotus Sutra,* and making music with percussion instruments such as bokken (Japanese castanets) and mallets.

In the opinion of anthropologist Carmen Blacker,* these "possessions" may be an unconscious protest against Japanese society's deeply ingrained gender discrimination. Most of the "patients," in fact, are women, and the same is true in several East African societies. The course of possession and exorcism among some Tanzanian women is especially revealing. One of the symptoms that a woman is possessed is that she begins wearing men's clothing. The cure involves having a female exorcist come to live with the victim for a few weeks. Anthropologists suggest that this improves the woman's situation by making her the center of attention within the household, and causing her husband to treat her better.

* Quoted in Mircea Eliade, ed., The Encyclopedia of Religion (New York: Macmillan, 1987).

* * *

How Do Chameleons Change Color to Match Their Background?

* * *

*T*hey don't. Chameleons do change color, but they have a limited range—brown, gray, and green, usually—and they can't match patterns. They won't become invisible sitting on your plaid skirt or paisley tie. Even many solid colors are beyond their abilities. "Attempts to induce these reptiles to turn red, blue, or black by placing them on the appropriately colored background are bound to be disappointing," says authority Hilda Simon.*

---

* *Chameleons and Other Quick-Change Artists* (New York: Dodd Mead, 1973).

Even in its natural environment, the chameleon won't always blend with the brown twigs or green leaves it's perched among. The surrounding temperature, light intensity, and background color all affect a chameleon's hue, according to University of Arizona researchers Joseph Bagnara and Mac Hadley.

Still, camouflage is useful to chameleons, because the lizards have no other defense against predators. Besides, it helps them lie in wait invisibly for the insects they eat. Nevertheless, ac-

cording to Simon, the main cause of color changes in chameleons seems to be "expression of moods and emotions."

Normally, unless frightened, chameleons that live in forests begin the day with a light, tawny brown color, which gradually darkens or turns to a dull green. (Desert-dwelling species, on the other hand, fade to a lighter, reflective hue as the temperature rises.) When startled, most chameleons flush to bright green or nearly black. This rapid, dramatic change may confuse or frighten a predator long enough to permit escape. A chameleon may even change color to express "triumph" after defeating another in a fight, says Simon.

How does it work? The secret is chromatophores—special skin cells whose name means "carriers of color." They contain pigment granules that sometimes disperse throughout the cell, and at other times concentrate in its center. For example, in one kind of color cell, the melanophore ("carrier of blackness"), dispersal of the pigment makes the cell turn black, whereas concentration makes it transparent.

A typical color-changing animal (and there are many, including the flounder, the squid, and some frogs, as well as the chameleon) might have a layer of yellow-colored cells near the surface of the skin; melanophores beneath them; and under those, iridophores, which produce a blue tint by refracting or scattering light, as the earth's atmosphere does. When the pigment in the melanophores is dispersed, the resulting yellow-over-black pattern makes the animal look brown. When the granules of pigment are concentrated, however, the black layer becomes clear, making the yellow and blue layers visible, yielding a green color.

The mechanism that triggers this movement of pigment granules differs greatly from species to species. For example, in chameleons, electrical impulses in the nervous system control color change, but in some other lizards, chemicals dispersed in the body by the hormonal system, especially the pituitary and pineal glands in the head, cause the effect.

If you buy a "chameleon" at an American pet store, you may actually be getting an anole instead. Both species are lizards and both can change color, but they have little else in common. Anoles are six to eight inches long and resemble those sleek, fast lizards you often see sunning themselves on rocks. Chameleons, on the other hand, are larger (ranging up to two feet long), have wrinkled skin, and have bodies that are higher than they are wide, like a leaf standing on edge—a means of camouflage when the animal is standing on a leafy branch. A chameleon's tongue is as long as the rest of its body, and is controlled by two sets of muscles—one to flick it out and another to bring it back (preferably with a tasty bug attached to its sticky tip).

Medieval Europeans thought that chameleons lived on nothing but air. (Shakespeare referred to that belief in *Hamlet*.) In fact, they eat mostly insects, but some of the larger species even eat small birds.

* * *

Was Eve's Apple a Red Delicious, a Granny Smith, or a Macintosh?

* * *

Almost certainly it wasn't an apple at all. The authors of Genesis, who lived in Palestine between twenty-five hundred and three thousand years ago, never saw an apple. The Hebrew word they used in the story of Eden was a generic term for fruit. They were, after all, more interested in the theological symbolism of the story than in the taxonomical classification of some prehistoric snack.

Biblical translators from Saint Jerome (Latin, circa A.D. 400)

to Martin Luther and William Tyndale (German and English, 1500s) to the scholars of the *Biblia de Jerusalén* (Spanish, twentieth century) have consistently rendered the word as *fruit* in their own languages, as did John Milton in *Paradise Lost*.

But the identification of the fruit as an apple, in the English language anyway, goes back to the dawn of English literature. The Old English poet Caedmon, whose work was handed down orally for three centuries before being written down in about A.D. 1000, called Eve's fruit an apple. So have many paraphrasers of the biblical story since then.

In English, though, *apple* has been used to mean fruit in general for at least as long as it has specifically meant the fruit of the genus *Malus* (a member of the rose family). The confusion of Eden's fruit with the apple, then, is as old as the English language itself.

Just for the sake of argument, let's make the very improbable assumption that the authors of Genesis *were* familiar with the apple. Eden was supposed to have been located somewhere east of Palestine; the apple seems to have originated somewhat farther east, around the Caspian Sea. So, if we wildly speculate that apples were growing in the area where the authors of Genesis thought Eden had been located, at the time the book was written, *then* what kind of apples would they have been?

Probably not any variety we'd recognize. According to an authoritative source,* the apple hybridizes easily. Whatever the earliest apples were like, their kind probably doesn't exist today.

The apple as we know it today, then, didn't cause the Fall of Man. But can an apple a day keep the doctor away? Maybe, if your complaint is gastrointestinal: The fiber in apples can serve both as a laxative and as a diarrhea cure. But the apple is pretty lousy as a source of nutrition. It has very small amounts of vitamin A or C, and although it contains some potassium, bananas and even lettuce contain more. Half the nutrients an apple does have are in the skin. You can enjoy eating an apple without worrying that you're reenacting the original sin, but for keeping the doctor away, nothing beats a bumper sticker that says, I SUPPORT SOCIALIZED MEDICINE.

* Fred Lape, *Apples and Man* (New York: Van Nostrand Reinhold, 1979).

* * *

How Does Olive Oil Lose Its (Extra) Virginity?

* * *

It's not easy being extra-virgin olive oil. Any one of several missteps along the way can make it lose that designation and downgrade it to merely "pure."

What's so special about extra-virgin olive oil? The price, for one thing! A quick check of gourmet food stores in the authors' home town found extra-virgin olive oils for sale at up to thirty-nine dollars a quart. Part of the price no doubt is due to the snob appeal or the fancy glass bottle, but olive oil labeled EXTRA

VIRGIN does have to meet certain legal requirements that increase the cost of production.

To begin with, extra-virgin oil comes from handpicked olives. Mechanical harvesters may bruise the olives; moreover, handpicking allows the selection of individual olives at the proper degree of ripeness. Of course, handpicking is labor-intensive and more expensive than mechanical means.

After two or three days of drying to reduce the water content, the olives are cold-pressed—ground into a paste slowly, at room temperature. It's more efficient to press the olives rapidly between metal wheels, but the faster process generates heat, which can damage the product's flavor. The paste is then heated a bit to make it easily spreadable. Higher heat results in a larger yield of oil, but again, heat is the enemy of good flavor. So for extra-virgin oil the heat is kept to a minimum, reducing the amount of oil extracted and thus again increasing the cost. The paste is spread on hemp mats. These are stacked into a giant sandwich which is then squashed to release the oil. The liquid may be centrifuged to separate out any remaining water.

Even after all this careful and expensive processing, the oil cannot be labeled EXTRA VIRGIN unless it contains less than 1 percent oleic acid (a fatty acid that can damage the taste) and passes tests for flavor, aroma, and color. The oil may then be bottled as is, or allowed to sit for six months so the solid particles will settle out, or filtered through cotton sheets to remove the solid matter immediately.

Oil that has been produced according to the regulations, but that doesn't quite pass the final inspection, can be sold under the name *superfine virgin* or just plain *virgin* olive oil. One brand advertises: "If it doesn't say 'Pompeian,' it's probably not *virgin* olive oil." True enough, since there aren't many brands of this particular grade, but the ad seems to imply that the term *virgin* denotes the best oil—which the informed consumer may consider an insult to his or her intelligence. (Pompeian now offers an extra virgin oil.)

The next grade down is "pure" olive oil. This blend is often the result of treating the once-pressed olive paste with a chemical solvent (which is evaporated later in the process), or heating the paste, and then pressing it a second and third time. It may also come from less-carefully harvested olives or from a first pressing at higher heat than is allowed for the better grades. "Pure" olive oil usually contains about 10 percent extra-virgin oil added at the end of processing to strengthen the flavor.

Some brands of olive oil are called *Light*. There's no legal definition of this term. It can refer to the flavor or the color, or may just be the product-manager's idea of a good sales pitch. What it definitely doesn't refer to is the calories: All olive oil is 100 percent fat, and when it comes to calories, fat is fat is fat.

The term *virgin* (in reference to olive oil, at least) has had various meanings over the years before regulators wrote the current legal definition. The *Dictionary Royal* of 1719 defined "virgin Oyl" simply as "sweet or pure Oyl." In the mid-1800s, the English used the term in much the same sense as we use it today, to mean oil "obtained by gentle pressure in the cold." French chefs (of course) had a stricter definition: Virgin oil was only that "which *spontaneously* separates from the paste of crushed olives."

If you use expensive extra-virgin olive oil for sautéing or other high-temperature cooking, you may be sending your cash up in smoke. Remember, the reason the hoity-toity stuff is so expensive in the first place is that it was carefully produced with as little heat as possible. Cooking experts recommend using extra-virgin olive oil on cold foods—drizzled on salads, goat cheese, or pasta, or mixed with balsamic vinegar in a plate and sopped up with Italian bread—or adding it to sauces only near the end of cooking.

Why Is "Jaywalking" Called That?

* * *

Jay *is an almost five-hundred-year-old term meaning dullard or sim-* pleton. A hundred years ago, "jay town" was an American slang synonym for "hick town." So a jaywalker is someone who pulls the stupid stunt of walking across a street in a dangerous place or without watching where he's going. *Jay- walker* seems to have originated in Boston around 1917.

In many parts of the country, people regard jaywalking as a noncrime. Worrying about getting a ticket for jaywalking is regarded as being about as silly as worrying about being trampled by a horde of Bigfoots on their way to see Elvis live in concert. But Los Angeles police still take jaywalking seriously, handing out fifty-four-dollar tickets to offenders. *Los Angeles Times* columnist Robert A. Jones calls the enforcement of jaywalking laws "one of the curious anomalies of Southern California." Jones explains that after World War II, Los Angeles residents and civic leaders wanted to create the image of a law-abiding and friendly city. As part of this image polishing, an unwritten social contract took effect: Drivers would cheerfully yield to pedestrians at crosswalks if pedestrians would not jaywalk elsewhere. Twenty years ago, Jones says, people usually abided by this tacit agreement, and police ticketed those who didn't. Nowadays, though, drivers don't uphold their end of the bargain, and L.A.'s pedestrian death rate is no lower than any other city's—but the jaywalking tickets still flow like California wine.

Jones investigated the history of jaywalking after getting a ticket himself in 1992. He described the scene of his crime: "I'm sure [passing rubberneckers] identified it quickly as a jaywalking bust. Everyone knows the signs, right? The bustee stands next to the officer without benefit of automobile or motorcycle nearby, looking faintly ridiculous."

Scotland Yard conducted an experiment in jaywalking prevention in 1967, setting up guardrails and increasing police supervision of pedestrians at one hundred fifty dangerous London intersections. The result: A 12-percent reduction in accidents. Now that the world's most legendary police force has gotten involved in foiling these heinous crimes, we can't understand why we haven't yet seen an Agatha Christie mystery entitled *The Case of the Jealous Jaywalker.*

* * *

Why Do Courts Impose Sentences of "Thirty Days or Thirty Dollars" When No One in His Right Mind Would Choose the Thirty Days?

* * *

The sentence isn't really as ridiculous as it sounds. "While in some sense the 'choice' of penalty is left to the defendant, this type of sentence is usually meant to be a fine, and the jail 'alternative' serves merely as an enforcement device to be used by the court only if necessary," according to a National Institute of Justice study of fines in sentencing.

Actually, the jail time isn't quite that long for such a small fine, even though the "30/30" formula has been repeated by judges in innumerable Western movies. In New York City today, for example, the alternative to a fine of thirty dollars is usually a week or less in the slammer. Some states have a dollars-to-days ratio set by statute; others let the judge decide the numbers.

In the United States, politicians who want to look like they're doing something about crime have demanded longer prison sentences for miscreants. (In one goofy but memorable television commercial, a candidate slammed a jail door shut to illustrate his anticrime proposals. The ad, at least, seems to have worked, whether or not the proposals did: The former candidate is now in his third term as Governor of his state.) As a result, American courts aren't as likely to impose fines alone as some other countries' judges are.

Still, U.S. laws use fines to keep malefactors from profiting from their crimes, or to force evildoers to reimburse society. Especially when there's a large fine, it makes sense to let a nonviolent convict remain at large so he can earn enough money to pay his debt, but the court often imposes probation or a suspended jail sentence to make sure the bad guy doesn't forget to send his monthly check.

Do Theaters Have a Prompter to Whisper Lines to Actors?

*M*any do, although nowadays, the prompter usually doesn't sit inside a shell at the front of the stage as depicted in so many cartoons. A century-old illustration of the Paris Opera shows the traditional shell, but today, the prompter usually stands in the wings.

Reminding actors of forgotten lines is only a very minor part of the prompter's job. Typically, this person is called the assistant stage manager, and may be responsible during performances for such things as ensuring that props are ready when needed, raising and lowering the curtain, and setting off fake thunder and lightning effects. In the old Metropolitan Opera House in New York, there was an imposing roomful of switches and levers, under the stage, for such purposes. But the prompter needs to be available to handle last-minute emergencies, such as locating a lost prop, and it's much easier to do so from the wings than from under the stage or in the isolated shell.

In smaller troupes, the prompter may also be a bit player or understudy, and most of the prompting actually takes place during rehearsals. Some directors (Noel Coward was among them) don't like to have actors reading from scripts even during the earliest rehearsals; but until the actors know their lines by heart, they may need frequent prompts. To ask for a line, the actor may say *line,* or may simply snap his or her fingers. Other directors prefer to use scripts, to prevent the disruption of frequent prompts during rehearsals, and also to keep actors from getting in the finger-snapping habit. It may confuse and annoy the audience if an actor unconsciously snaps his fingers while trying to remember a line during a performance.

For times when an actor really does need a prompt on stage, this textbook advice is offered: "Prompts should never be whispered; they should be spoken loudly and clearly. During performances, whispered prompts will be heard in the last row, but when they are spoken in a low voice, they will not reach the first row."*

The information a prompter gives an actor on stage is probably much more useful, and more welcome, than the vague advice directors sometimes give. During intermission at one play, for example, director Laurence Olivier went backstage and told Charlton Heston, "Be better."

---

* Roy A. Beck, et al., *Play Production Today!* (Skokie, Ill.: National Textbook Co., 1983).

* * *

Can Flashing Lights Induce an Epileptic Seizure?

* * *

Only about 2 to 5 percent of people with epilepsy are sensitive to flashing lights or other visual stimuli, such as lines of type on a page, or patterns of tile on a floor. This works out to something on the order of a couple of million people worldwide. The mechanism by which flashes cause seizures is "incompletely understood," wrote Dr. Gerald C. McIntosh of Colorado's Poudre Valley Hospital in a recent article on the subject.*

---

* In Thomas L. Bennett, ed., *The Neurophysiology of Epilepsy* (New York: Plenum, 1992).

However, researchers have come up with many practical ways to prevent such visually induced seizures.

An epileptic seizure does not always involve falling down and thrashing around. Its effects may be as apparently mild as staring and turning pale for a few seconds—a type of seizure known as the "typical absence." Or it can be somewhere in between. The seizure may cause a quick contraction of an arm or leg muscle—the so-called flying-saucer syndrome, because it tends to happen early in the morning when you may have just picked up your cup and saucer for breakfast coffee.

In photosensitive patients (that is, people in whom flashing lights can induce seizures), ten to twenty flashes per second is the frequency most likely to cause a seizure, although the range varies among individuals. The sun's reflection on rippling water, or alternating light and shadow caused by traveling quickly past trees, can produce the same effect.

Watching television can be risky for people with photosensitive epilepsy, because a TV broadcast consists of a quickly changing series of still pictures flashed onto the screen—thirty per second in the American TV system, twenty-five under the format used in some other countries. British epilepsy researchers A. Wilkins and Janet Lindsay recommend watching the telly in a darkened room, on a small screen (ten inches or less in diagonal measure), and not sitting very close to the screen, to reduce the possibility of a television-induced seizure. (Using a remote control can help the viewer avoid getting too close.)

Watching television with one eye also greatly reduces the chance of seizure. But it's a strain to keep one eye closed while watching a show, and if you put a patch over one eye, you lose the benefit of two-eyed vision when you get up during a commercial to go get another beer from the refrigerator. So an ingenious inventor came up with TV glasses: a pair of spectacles with one lens polarized vertically, and one horizontally. If you also put a vertically polarized piece of glass in front of the TV screen, the television picture will get through to one eye only—but you can still see everything else with both eyes.

The ancient Romans knew about visually induced seizures: Apuleius, writing in the second century, said that a spinning potter's wheel could be used as a diagnostic test for epilepsy. Modern observation and experimentation on the disorder dates from 1881 (effect of bright light) and 1927 (effect of flicker).

In 1981, medical journals began to report a new type of photosensitivity—*Space Invader* or "video game" epilepsy. In the first such case,* a seventeen-year-old boy experienced feelings of *déjà vu* (a frequent symptom of an impending seizure) and a grand-mal attack (loss of consciousness, falling down, and other pronounced symptoms) after finishing a game of *Astro Fighter.* This particular video machine displayed a flashing effect at the end of a game at the rate of sixteen flashes per second—well within the most dangerous range.

But rapidly flashing screens aren't the only culprit in video-game epilepsy. Some players do just fine until they get to a particular scene in a game. The "bricks" scene in *Super Mario Brothers,* for example, caused seizures in one player, even though the rest of the game had no effect on him. Researchers think that geometric patterns may also induce seizures in some patients. Since 1992, some video-game makers have included warnings in their instruction manuals about possible seizures.

A few people with photosensitive epilepsy have an urge to give themselves seizures deliberately. These tend to be children (girls more often than boys) who are relatively slow in mental development. They may wave their outspread fingers in front of their face, or jump up and down in front of a venetian blind, to induce seizures. Sometimes they explain that the result feels

---

* " 'Space Invader' Epilepsy," *The Lancet,* February 28, 1981.

good, but even in cases where the children don't report plea-surable sensations, punishment fails to stop the behavior. Why do it if it doesn't feel good? One researcher* speculated that the children might be using it as a means of escape from unpleasant situations, or as a cry for attention.

Some people can have a seizure when looking at a page of a book with its alternating pattern of lines of black type and white space. There's an invention that can help them: the *Cambridge Easy Reader,* a sheet of darkened plastic with a cutout window big enough to show only about three lines of text at a time.

It's not only visual stimuli that can cause seizures. If a word is repeated to a photosensitive patient while a seizure-inducing light is flashing, eventually, the word itself may cause a seizure. And some people, immune to the flashing light, may have problems with specific sounds. French composer Hector Ber-lioz, for example, suffered a seizure every time he heard a particular piece of music.

* Stephen L. Sherwood, *Archives of Neurology,* 1962.

Does the Tasmanian Devil Really Exist?

A lot of Australian ranchers and farmers wish the Tasmanian devil didn't exist, but it does. Although it's not quite as voracious as the character in the Bugs Bunny cartoons who eats "hogs, dogs, goats, stoats, bats, cats . . . and *especially* rabbits," the scientific name of its genus, *Sarcophilus,* should tip you off to the fact that it's no vegetarian: The word means "flesh lover" in Greek. Its diet includes birds, small mammals (watch out, Bugs!), and other live animals up to the size of a wallaby (a two- to three-foot-tall relative of the kangaroo), as well as dead meat.

The Tasmanian devil is a member of the marsupial order of mammals. Like all marsupials, Tasmanian devils give birth prematurely, after only one month of pregnancy. The tiny, blind young must grope their way to the mother's nipples, where they hang on for five more months, drinking milk, until they are fully developed. Like most marsupials, the Tasmanian devil has a pouch covering the teats. The order originated in the Americas, where some of its members (such as opossums) still live. But Australia has the most diverse collection of marsupials, including kangaroos and koalas as well as the Tasmanian devil.

The *Tasmanian* part of its name comes from the island of Tasmania, named for the Dutch explorer Abel Tasman, who, in 1642, became the first European to see the island. (For two hundred years, the place was called Van Diemen's Land, after another explorer, and if the name hadn't been changed, perhaps the animal would have been christened "Van Diemen's Demon.") The Tasmanian devil is found today only on Tasmania, but it also lived on the continent of Australia until it became extinct there in the twentieth century, a loser in an ecological competition with the dingo.

The Satanic half of the name was bestowed by British settlers who hated the snarling little predator who "raised hell" with their chickens and sheep.

The creature is a little smaller than the average dog, and with its brown-and-black fur and pointed snout, it looks like a little bear with stumpy legs, or a big fuzzy rat.

By the way, the animal that looks like a striped dog, which you may have seen pictured on the label of Boag's, a Tasmanian brand of beer, is the Tasmanian *wolf*. It is not related to the devil, and is thought to be extinct. People in Tasmania also call it the Tasmanian tiger or hyena, and the beer itself is colloquially known simply as "Two Dogs."

* * *

Why Do Beans Give You Gas, but Cucumbers Make You Burp?

* * *

Here's evidence of the power of advertising. Seed companies promote "burpless" cucumbers, so everyone assumes that other varieties of cucumber *make* you burp. While it's true that some cucumbers can cause stomach *upset* in some people, neither the cucumber nor any other food causes increased stomach gas or belching, according to Martin H. Floch of Yale University. Except in individuals with certain diseases, burps are caused exclusively by swallowing air.

After originating in Japan, the so-called burpless cucumber was introduced into the United States, ironically, by the Burpee Seed Company. The variety, also called the Japanese trellis cucumber, is different from the standard American "slicer," says Todd C. Wehner, a plant geneticist at North Carolina State University. The standard slicer is easier to ship because of its thick skin. The Japanese trellis variety is longer, thinner-skinned, milder-flavored, and does seem to produce less stomach upset in people susceptible to that problem.

Until recently, scientists suspected that "burpless" cucumbers were less irritating to the stomach than other varieties because they lacked a gene that makes cucumbers bitter. (Some kinds of wild cucumber are known to have an "extra-bitter" gene, which makes them unattractive to pests, and which is bred out of cultivated cucumbers.) Recent tests by Ken Owens of the Petoseed company, however, have shown that even "burpless" cucumbers carry the regular bitter gene, despite their milder flavor. So it's still unknown just what genetic trait makes for a cucumber that reduces stomach irritation.

Although cucumbers do not cause you to burp, the part of the question dealing with beans is still valid.

"Beans, beans, they're good for your heart . . ." may or may not be sound medical advice, but the next line of that children's rhyme is definitely true. Everyone has some gas in the intestines, from swallowed air that's not expelled by burping before it passes beyond the stomach, and from absorption of nitrogen from the blood. Typically, the human colon (large or lower intestine) contains an amount of gas that occupies about one hundred cubic centimeters at normal air pressure, but which can expand seven-fold at the pressure found at altitudes of forty thousand feet. This, says physiologist Horace W. Davenport of the University of Michigan, gives "the informed [airline] passenger something to think about besides the technique of adjusting an oxygen mask" when the flight attendant speaks of "the unlikely event of a drop in cabin pressure." Ouch.

Certain foods, though, can cause the production of much larger amounts of gas in the intestine. Beans are particularly troublesome because they contain types of fiber, such as stachyose and raffinose, known collectively as oligosaccharides. The digestive enzymes in the human stomach cannot break down these molecules, but certain bacteria found in the colon can. The result is hydrogen gas. Most of this gas, along with the nitrogen, carbon dioxide, methane, and other gases in the intestine, are expelled during one of approximately fourteen daily "flatus events," as medical science euphemistically calls them. But a fraction of the hydrogen is reabsorbed into the blood stream, deposited in the lungs, and exhaled.

Beans can increase production of intestinal gas by 500 percent over a bean-free diet, but other foods cause gas, too. Apple and prune juices produce lots of hydrogen; grape juice, bananas, and Brussels sprouts produce some, as does lactose (found in milk) in people who are deficient in lactase (the enzyme that digests it); but orange juice and apricot nectar produce very little gas.

Flatus (intestinal gas) containing hydrogen and methane will "burn with a hard, gem-like flame," according to Davenport, and are potentially explosive. Patients preparing for certain types of surgery, therefore, must go on a low-fiber diet, take laxatives and enemas, and have their nether regions suffused with non-inflammable carbon dioxide gas. When these safety precautions have been omitted, patients have been killed or injured by gas explosions during the cauterization of polyps in their intestines. In one case, described by Minneapolis physician John H. Bond,* a seventy-one-year-old man was having a polyp removed when a loud explosion hurled the doctor against the

* *Gastrointestinal Endoscopy*, 1976.

wall. The sigmoidoscope was filled with black smoke and shredded tissue. But the patient, who reported feeling no pain,
merely cautioned, "You know, a doctor could get hurt doing
that!" (He recovered after surgery to repair the damage.) In
another case reported by Dallas physician H. Gray Carter in
1952,* a blue flame shot one or two feet out of the sigmoidoscope.

* American Journal of Surgery, 1952.

Why Do We Say That Someone Who Escapes Punishment Goes "Scot-Free"?

In the thirteenth century, scot *was the word for money you would pay* at a tavern for food and drink, or when they passed the hat to pay the entertainer. Later, it came to mean a local tax that paid the sheriff's expenses. "To go scot-free" literally meant to be exempted from paying this tax. It had its figurative meaning by, at the latest, 1531, the year when translator William Tyndale published a commentary on the Bible in which he referred to God letting a "poor sinner . . . go scot-free."

The "scot" tax was an early form of the progressive tax—that is, a tax based on ability to pay. Thus, when President Ronald Reagan made the United States tax system less progressive in the 1980s, he was literally letting the rich go scot-free!

The etymology of the word *scot* is unclear, but, apparently, has nothing to do with Scotland or with the ethnic stereotype of Scots as being expenditure-challenged (or, to be very politically incorrect, cheap). The phrase "scot and lot" (or "scat and lot") refers to a different tax, this one imposed by towns to pay municipal expenses. To "pay someone off scot and lot" means to pay your debt in full. But "to scat and lot with someone" means "to go Dutch" or to split the cost of something evenly.

Then there's "Great Scott!"—which is only a little over a century old and has nothing to do with the scot tax, scot and lot, Scotland, or anyone named Scott. It's just a euphemism for the oath "Great God!" It's also, as any aficionado of *The Rocky Horror Picture Show* can tell you, what the audience shouts whenever Dr. von Scott appears on the screen.

* * *

Why Aren't There Any "Grade B" Eggs?

* * *

There aren't many Grade B eggs in your local grocery store because customers don't want to buy them. Edgar Ingram, egg-inspection supervisor with the North Carolina Department of Agriculture, explains:

> While it is true that nutritionally Grade A and Grade B may be of equal value, there is very little consumer demand for Grade B shell eggs. [Shell eggs are eggs still in their shells, as com-

pared to powdered eggs, frozen egg liquid, etc.] Consequently, Grade B eggs are sent to egg-products processing plants where they are used in the preparation of further processed products. At the present time, I know of no retail store, large or small, that carries Grade B eggs. Fifteen or twenty years ago, a few stores did stock them, but due to the slow movement, they were discontinued.

What's wrong with a Grade B egg that makes shoppers shun them? Not much but the name, apparently. If you want a perfect-looking poached or fried egg, then you should stick with Grades AA and A, which have firm, centered yolks and clear, thick whites. For scrambling, or making dough or batter, though, Grade B eggs would be just as good (if you could find them).

Some of the "defects" that can downgrade an egg to B status, according to California's Food and Agriculture Regulations, are: a "weak and watery" white; a yolk that is "clearly visible" through the shell, is enlarged or flattened, or has spots; stains on the shell; or an air cell bigger than one-quarter inch—the air cell inside a freshly laid egg is usually about one-eighth inch but gets bigger with time, so a larger air cell may indicate an older egg. An entire lot of eggs may be downgraded to B if more than a certain percentage of them are "leakers" or even "checks" (shells cracked but not leaking).

There's even one lower grade for eggs, Grade C, a kind of limbo just above the "inedible" classification. These may have blood clots or spots in the white (due to the development of an embryo), or air cells bigger than three-eighths inch. But any of the following will make an egg legally "inedible": an embryo so far along in development that there's a visible blood ring within the yolk; eggs with green whites; and eggs fitting any of the descriptions "black rots, yellow rots, white rots, mixed rots, or sour eggs."

Egg cartons will also tell you the size of the eggs, but this has nothing to do with the grade. Sizes range from Jumbo (about two and a half ounces each), through Extra Large, Large, Medium, and Small (one and a half ounces), down to a category with no minimum size, though if you ask your grocer for them, he may answer that he's got chicken eggs, and maybe even quail eggs, but no Peewee eggs.

* * *

How Did Hershey Make Those Heat-Resistant Desert Chocolate Bars for the Troops During the Persian Gulf War?

* * *

In August 1990, Iraqi troops invaded their southerly neighbor Kuwait, and shortly afterward, it was announced that Hershey Foods Corporation had developed a melt-proof chocolate bar for American troops hunkered down in Saudi Arabia. How did they make such a bar, and how did it compare with Hershey's regular chocolate bar?

We thought that first we'd learn a little about the history of chocolate, and about how chocolate is made, figuring it to be a very simple process. After all, you just throw a lot of sugar, some milk, some cocoa and a few other innocuous ingredients together, heat and stir it, and pour it in a mold, right? Wrong! Rocket fuel should be as hard to process!

Chocolate products are derived from the seeds of any of three varieties of the cacao tree (that's right—*cacao* tree, not *cocoa* tree—it's hypothesized that early English importers of the product goobered-up the spelling, and we've had it wrong ever since). These trees grow in a narrow equatorial band, with most of the predominant variety cultivated in West Africa and Brazil. The etymology of the word *cacao* is believed to be a Maya Indian phrase meaning "bitter juice." The Maya and Aztec Indians used the beans as currency, and to make a cold, unsweetened and therefore bitter drink called *cacahuatl*. Spanish explorers in the early 1500s heated and sweetened it with sugar, resulting in a drink the Indians named *chocolatl*. It was first brought to Europe, specifically Spain, by Hernán Cortés in 1528, and several decades later began to spread throughout Europe.

Cocoa beans grow inside pods, and have a shell that surrounds the usable portion of the bean—the nib. Pods are cut from the trees and opened; the beans are removed, covered with plantain leaves or burlap, and fermented for up to ten days, after which they are thoroughly dried, and then packaged for shipment. Interestingly, the beans have no chocolaty flavor prior to fermentation.

At the factory, the beans are cleaned, in a dry process, to remove sand and other waste; they are roasted to improve flavor and shake the nib loose from the shell; and then the shells are cracked and removed entirely by a complex winnowing machine.

Now we're ready to make cocoa powder. The nibs are ground and heated to the melting point of the cocoa butter they contain (which makes up more than half of the nib), and the resulting "chocolate liquor" has the bejabbers pressed out of it at several thousand pounds per square inch, causing it to express some of its cocoa butter. The solid cakes that remain are finely ground, and voilà—cocoa powder!

The various forms of chocolate (bitter chocolate, milk chocolate, and others) are also manufactured from "chocolate liquor," with other ingredients such as cocoa butter (extracted in the manufacture of cocoa powder), sugar, and milk solids added to the liquor as appropriate. The ingredients are mixed, and unpalatable natural substances are removed in a process called conching, both mixing and conching being preceded by tempering, which prevents some of the cocoa butter from crystallizing in an unsightly manner. Each of these processes is fairly complicated.

So, next time you feel like bitching about the cost of a chocolate bar, perhaps you should think twice, huh?! But back to the original question: What's the scoop on the desert bar?

We contacted Marsha Gardner, a Hershey public relations representative, who sent us a slew of information. It turns out that Hershey has been in the business of making chocolate bars for the military for decades, but not always with the same product goals.

In 1937, Army Quartermaster Captain Paul Logan met with Hershey officials to discuss commissioning the production of a field ration bar to meet the dietary needs of a soldier in a starvation situation during a global war. Presumably a chocolate bar was desired because the sugar and cocoa butter provide a lot of calories, and cocoa butter, which is a fat, has anti-rancidity properties that give it a shelf life of three to five years. The eventual result was known as the Logan Bar and later, Field Ration D. It met the original requirements: It weighed four ounces, was heat resistant, was high in calories, and had added Vitamin B1 (to prevent beriberi disease—of particular concern in tropical venues). But what was to keep soldiers from eating the chocolate bars for fun, instead of saving them for emergencies? Logan had told Hershey to make the bar taste "just a little better than a boiled potato." (It must be wonderful to be a food manufacturer, be approached by one of the world's largest and deepest-pocket consumers—the U.S. military—and be told to make a product that doesn't taste very good!)

The military was pleased, but Hershey had a desperate technical problem: Their new formula, by design, would not melt to a liquid, and all of their machinery required liquid flow. To meet the demand for ninety thousand test bars, Hershey actually pressed the chocolate paste into molds by hand. As World War II marched toward American involvement, Hershey developed the machinery to meet the impending production requirements.

Then the Japanese bombed Pearl Harbor, and Hershey's headaches returned. The military wanted poison-gas-proof packaging for many of its rations, and the requirements, as given in a Hershey pamphlet on the subject, were:

> . . . placing each bar in a heavy cellophane bag, closing the bag by means of heat seal, inserting this into an individual cardboard carton, securely gluing the carton ends, dipping the cartons in a wax mixture, packing twelve waxed cartons in a master carton, gluing the master cartons top and bottom, packing twelve master cartons in a wooden case, and nailing and steel stripping the case.

Cripes! Why not just seal the bars in a huge block of cement and open them with a grenade? In any event, Hershey was eventually producing twenty-four million ration bars a week, for an estimated output of three billion between 1940 and 1945. Among these bars was the newly developed Hershey's Tropical Chocolate Bar, which had improved chocolate taste at the military's request (one suspects that some field general tried a Field Ration D bar and had a hissy fit about the taste). They also produced the bars in packs of three, because such a pack would provide the 1,800 calories the military considered minimal daily intake for a soldier in combat. By 1945, Hershey was also producing the military's Emergency Accessory packet, Field Rations C and K, and the 10-in-1, Life Boat, Air Craft, and Prisoner of War Rations.

In September 1990, a month after the Iraqi invasion, the military asked Hershey to develop a bar from real milk chocolate that was heat resistant and as good as regular chocolate. The result, developed with Battelle Memorial Institute in Geneva, was first shipped to Saudi Arabia in December 1990: Hershey's Desert Bar. Regular milk chocolate melts at 78 degrees Fahrenheit, but the Desert Bar keeps its normal consistency up to 140 degrees, and never melts but only becomes "fudgey." The company even recommended sampling this consistency by microwaving the bar. Ms. Gardner told us the key to the bar is in the processing, not the ingredients. Indeed, the only ingredient unique to the Desert Bar is egg whites, which contain ovalbumin, a form of protein. Though we're not food chemists, we suspect this ingredient *is* important for heat resistance, but the company says it's not, and won't discuss *any* aspect of the bar's manufacturing. (There's an irony here: Most of the technology required to build a low-yield nuclear fission bomb has been de-classified for years and printed in the public domain, but try to find out how the army's chocolate bar is made and, whoa boy, watch out!)

In May 1991, Hershey announced the availability of the Desert Bar nationwide. However, the company says the bar is no longer distributed nationally, so we were unable to glean one for taste testing. One of our "moles" inside the company says he thinks they're developing a new version, which may explain why, though the bar is not available, Ms. Gardner declined to describe it as "discontinued."

* * *

Why Does Pointing the Index Finger at Someone and Rubbing the Other Index Finger Over It Mean "Shame on You"?

* * *

When a parent wants to discipline a child, or an adult wants to make an angry and direct statement to someone during an argument, they often point an index finger at the other person. The "shame on you" gesture, rubbing that finger with the index finger of the other hand, represents the *sharpening* of that "finger of scorn," as one might sharpen a pencil with a knife, according to Ernest Thompson Seton, author of an early study of sign language.*

---

* Ernest Thompson Seton, *Sign Talk* (Garden City: Doubleday, 1918).

Seton's book lists many sign-language gestures used by the Plains Indians, and many more from the language of the deaf, but this "shame on you" gesture is not among either of those vocabularies. It does appear in his list of one hundred fifty gestures common among American children at the time the book was written, early in this century, but it is labeled as being "popular" in origin, rather than part of any particular system of sign language.

The gesture dates back hundreds of years. In medieval paintings of Christ's Passion, mocking onlookers are frequently shown sharpening their fingers at Jesus, other authorities point out.*

There seems to be no single English word for this sign, although people often say *tsk tsk* in connection with it. The Germans, however, do have a word for it: *Rübenschaben,* which literally means "to pare a turnip" at someone.

Deaf people use several gestures for *shame* in their sign language. Instead of pointing a sharpened finger, though, they use signs that refer to the blushing that accompanies shame: a cupped hand placed next to the cheek with a twist of the wrist, or two fingers drawn down the cheek. The Chinese use a similar gesture.

---

* Betty and Franz Bäuml, *A Dictionary of Gestures* (Metuchen, NJ: Scarecrow Press, 1975).

What's the Difference Between a Troll and an Ogre, or a Fairy and a Pixie, or a Goblin and a Hobgoblin?

Some of the words for mythical supernatural beings are generic, while others refer to specific types of good or evil spirits, or even to single individuals. The words *sprite* and *fairy* are the most general, referring to any spirit with power over mortals' lives. *Sprite* in fact comes from the same root as the word *spirit; fairy* comes from the Latin *fata,* the Fates.

As we get more specific, we'll start at the good end of the spectrum of fairies and work our way through the mischievous

ones all the way to the truly heinous. *Nixies* are water-dwelling humanoid creatures whose name comes from Greek and Germanic roots meaning *to wash;* the Old High German words for hippopotamus and crocodile are related to *nixie. Mermaids* and underwater *nymphs* are examples of nixies. Not all nymphs live in the water, though.

With a name based on the Greek word for bride, all nymphs are female, and come in many varieties. A *dryad* is a nymph who lives in the woods; a *hamadryad* is associated with an individual tree and lives only as long as the tree lives; and *oreads* are mountain nymphs. Aquatic nymphs include *naiads,* who live in rivers or springs; and the salt-water species *nereids* and *oceanids,* daughters of the sea gods Nereus and Oceanus, respectively.

The pointy-hatted little *pixie* (the word comes from southwestern England but its origin is obscure) may be the only kind of fairy ever to be discussed at a United States Senate committee hearing. On April 29, 1954, the red-baiting Senator Joseph McCarthy (Republican from Wisconsin) was conducting a witch-hunt for alleged Communists in the U.S. Army. Assisting McCarthy was the notorious lawyer Roy Cohn. Opposing them was the Army's counsel, Joseph Welch. Part of the sparring that day concerned a piece of evidence, a photograph, that Welch suspected McCarthy of having doctored. Welch got the best of McCarthy (who, like Cohn, was rumored to be a homosexual) with the following exchange:

WELCH: Did you think this came from a pixie? Where did you think that this picture I hold in my hand came from?

McCARTHY: Will counsel for my benefit define—I think he might be an expert on this—what a pixie is?

WELCH: Yes, I should say, Mr. Senator, that a pixie is a close relative of a fairy. Shall I proceed, sir? Have I enlightened you?

Historian Fred J. Cook described the reaction: "Laughter shook the hearing room. Roy Cohn's lips tightened into white angry lines, and McCarthy glowered in his fury."*

The *leprechaun* is another kind of benign fairy; he lives in Ireland, makes shoes, and owns a pot of gold, which you can have *if* you can catch him. But if he can trick you into taking your eyes off him for just a moment, he will disappear before revealing the gold's hiding place. The word comes from the Irish for *small body.*

Next, we'll meet some fairies who aren't quite as nice to be around as a beautiful dryad or a wealthy leprechaun. *Goblins* are "mischievous and ugly," according to the *Oxford English Dictionary;* the word may come from the Greek *kobalos,* which means *rogue.* One particular goblin is the *hobgoblin,* whom you may know better as Puck, the Shakespearean character who says, "Lord, what fools these mortals be!" The Bard didn't invent Puck; he was well known in medieval England (and also Ireland and Wales, where he was called *pooka* or *pwcca*) as a spirit specializing in spoiling milk and misleading lost travelers at night. Another name for him was Robin Goodfellow, or, for short, Rob or Hob—voilà, *hobgoblin,* which is not a type of spirit, but a name for a single individual, Puck.

One of the most recently invented fairy creatures is the *gremlin,* a mischievous, destructive little guy who enforced Murphy's Law on Royal Air Force planes during World War II. No one knows exactly what the word means; it started appearing in British fliers' slang in the early 1940s.

Trolls and *ogres* are both nasty creatures. In Scandinavian folklore, trolls were originally giants, but later were represented as dwarfish. They only come out at night, because sunlight will turn them to stone. Some of them live under bridges,

---

* Fred J. Cook, *The Nightmare Decade* (New York: Random House, 1971).

where they make travelers pay tolls or perform difficult feats before being allowed to cross. They also appear in the folklore of islands off Scotland, where they're called *trows*. Ogres, man-eating giants, come from more southerly cultures such as France and Spain. One possible origin of the word *ogre* is the Greek *Orcus,* another name for the god of the underworld, also known as Hades and Pluto. Readers of J. R. R. Tolkien will probably be reminded of the evil ''orcs'' in his books. But it's not clear whether the word *ogre* is at all related to *orca,* the name for the so-called killer whale. *Orca* was the Latin word for some kind of whale, but it wasn't necessarily derived from *Orcus.*

At last, we get to the truly diabolical spirits. *Demons* didn't start out as evil, but over time, they acquired that connotation. In Greek mythology, a *daimon* (also spelled *daemon*) was a spirit ranking somewhere between man and the gods, often the ''genius'' or indwelling spirit of a particular place. The word began to go bad when the enemies of Socrates accused him of being guided by a personal daimon; in fact, he had said only that he obeyed a *daimonion,* or guiding principle, not some kind of possessing spirit. Early Christian writers such as Augustine and the translators of the Septuagint Bible used the Latin word *daemon* similarly to mean an evil spirit, and the connotation has stuck to this day. In Australian slang, police were called ''demons,'' possibly from the old name for Tasmania, Van Diemen's Land (for more on this, revisit the Tasmanian devil in an earlier chapter).

Another diabolical spirit is the *imp,* from the Greek word for graft or sapling. More generally, it means the child of someone, but the *someone* is usually the Devil. Imps often serve as witches' familiar spirits.

Finally come the evil spirits who can't get their minds out of the gutter. You have your choice of two kinds—well, actually, you don't have a choice at all, since they get you while you sleep. The *incubus* (Latin for "he who lies upon") and *succubus* ("she who lies underneath") seduce sleepers, usually but not always of the opposite sex. Sometimes, though, they just cause nightmares. That must be on the nights when they have a headache.

In addition to slipping into unsuspecting sleepers' beds, these randy spirits can also show up under the magnifying glass in the staid environment of a botany lab. Scientists classify liverworts (plants related to mosses and buttercups) as either incubous or succubous—note the spelling; these are adjectives—depending on whether the older leaves lie on top of or underneath the younger ones.

* * *

What's the Difference Between Blackheads and Whiteheads, and Why Do Teenagers Get Such Bad Cases of Them?

* * *

Blackheads and whiteheads are just different stages of the same thing. The generic term is *comedone* (pronounced COH-mi-dohn), from the Latin word meaning both "glutton" and "worm of the kind that eats corpses." Obviously not a good thing to have bustin' out all over your face.

When a child reaches puberty, her ovaries and adrenal glands, or his testes, begin to produce the hormone androgen, one of whose effects is to enlarge the sebaceous glands, which surround hairs and secrete oil, to moisturize the skin through the hair follicle. If a gland is blocked, the bacterium *Propionibacterium acnes,* which thrives in fat-rich and oxygen-free environments, begins to multiply and irritate the gland. The irritation leads to the increased production of keratin, or horn cells, which form a comedone whose tip is visible as a blackhead. Washing won't make it go away; the color comes from concentrated melanin in the horn cells.

If the mouth of the follicle becomes blocked at the surface of the skin, the gland becomes distended, triggering an immune-system reaction, and the area begins to fill with pus, visible as a whitehead.

While a dermatologist can open and drain whiteheads therapeutically, you should not stand in front of a mirror and try to pop your own zits. It can cause the sebaceous gland to rupture beneath the skin and infect other glands, just making things worse. Popped zits around the forehead and nose can even drain into the sinuses, causing problems much more dangerous than acne itself. Besides, all that gunk splattered all over the mirror is just gross.

Why Is the Playing Card with the Young Man's Face Called a "Jack"?

The picture is supposed to represent either a soldier or a servant, and the card was originally called the *knave,* from German *Knabe,* which means boy. (Remember the knave of hearts who stole the queen's tarts?) In many other European languages it's called something that suggests one of these two roles: in German, *Bube* (another word for boy); in French and Russian, *valet;* in Italian, *fante* (infantryman).

In Spanish, the card corresponding to the jack is called *la sota* (a derogatory term for a woman, translated variously as hussy, slut, bitch). The picture on the card, though, is that of a page boy or a young person of indeterminate gender. The *sota* may originally have represented either a courtesan or a princess. (The Spanish deck is unlike the English one in other ways as well: Each of its four suits has cards worth 1 through 7; skipping 8 and 9, it continues with the sota, worth 10; the horse, worth 11; and the king, worth 12.)

The English card term *jack* is at least three hundred years old. But in 1861, when Charles Dickens wrote *Great Expectations,* "jack" was apparently regarded as a lower-class slang name for the card, as this passage suggests: " 'He calls the knaves, jacks, this boy,' said Estella with disdain. . . . 'And what coarse hands he has! And what thick boots.' "

Apparently, the word comes from the custom of using *Jack,* a nickname for the very common name *John,* to refer to any generic, run-of-the-mill man, as in the phrase "every man Jack of them," or the practice of addressing a man you don't know by saying, "Hey, Jack!" Unlike the other two face cards in the deck, the king and the queen, the knave is nobody royal or special; he's just your average Jack.

The nursery rhyme "Jack and Jill" has nothing to do with playing cards, but hey, we *are* talking about Jacks here. As with so many seemingly silly or innocuous nursery rhymes, some scholars claim there's a political and economic message behind it. In England, for many centuries, a "gill" (pronounced *jill,* and derived from the Latin *gellus,* a wine glass) was a unit of liquid measure. A jack was half a gill. The government under King Charles I (reigned 1625–49), in an effort to sneak a "sin tax" increase past the public, reduced the officially defined size of the gill, without changing the amount of tax charged per gill of wine. (Sort of like modern candy manufacturers, who shrink the size of the chocolate bar without lowering the price.) So when the nursery rhyme's Jack falls down, and Jill comes tumbling after, they represent the fall or decrease in the size of the standard measures of wine and the relation between them: When one falls, the other one, by definition, tumbles, too.

There are several other explanations of the rhyme, including other political allegories as well as a Freudian interpretation (a boy and a girl are playing together, spill some liquid, and fall down—hmm). One researcher even puts forward the radical theory that the rhyme is just a cute little singsong poem about a couple of kids, with no deeper meaning. Imagine that.

Why Do Churches Have Steeples?

***

*D*oesn't everybody *know that the steeple is supposed to draw the* viewer's attention heavenward, that the church *spire* is supposed to lead people to *aspire* to heaven? Like a lot of things that "everybody knows," that belief is at best a partial truth, but not the whole story, with a bit of outright misinformation sprinkled in.

In fact, the development of the steeple has a lot more to dowith rampaging Visigoths, Emperor Charlemagne, abandoned Roman babies, and leaky roofs, than with religious symbolism.

Before we get to the fun stuff like the Sack of Rome, though, we need to get our terminology in order. To be very technical about it, the steeple is the tower, usually square, that supports the spire, the tapering, often octagonal, structure on top. But in general usage, *steeple* can refer to the combination of tower and spire. The word *steeple* is related to *steep*. *Spire* comes from Germanic words for spear, and refers to the long, thin, pointed shape of the structure. *Spire* most definitely does *not* have anything to do with *aspire,* which comes from the Latin word for breath and is related to the word spirit. The only connection between *spire* and *aspire* is that they rhyme. And a *belfry* originally not only had nothing to do with bells, but didn't even sound as if it did. The word used to be *berfrey,* apparently from the Greek words for portable tower, which, in the Middle Ages, is what the word meant: a movable wooden tower from which an attacking army could besiege a fortified city. Similar wooden structures on or near buildings came to be called *berfreys* too, and since they often contained a church's bells, popular confusion corrupted the word to *belfry.*

Now, back to the Roman Empire, and the fascinating history of the steeple as told by historian Sartell Prentice.* In the earliest days of Christianity, one could join the Church merely by professing one's faith and being baptized. But when Rome made Christianity its state religion in the fourth century, the Church became increasingly bureaucratic, and its theological doctrines became more elaborate. The Church began to require that its catechumens (aspiring members) undergo months or even years of instruction in the faith before baptism. But only baptized Christians were allowed to enter church buildings themselves, so where were these classes to take place? The

---

* Sartell Prentice, *The Heritage of the Cathedral* (New York: William Morrow and Co., 1936).

solution was the atrium, a colonnaded area between the street and the church, where converts could be instructed and the intellectually curious could ask church members about their religion.

No steeples yet. Bear with us.

In ancient Rome, women often dealt with unwanted pregnancies by abandoning infants on the street. Entrepreneurs would gather these babies and sell them as slaves or gladiators. To save them from this fate, the Church took many abandoned children under its protection and baptized them.

The practice of baptizing infants who didn't even know their own names, much less understand the catechism, made the requirement of a long educational process for adult converts look illogical. So did mass instant conversions of whole Germanic tribes whose chieftains converted to Christianity (often for political and military reasons) and ordered their subjects to go along.

As the requirement of long theological training for converts died out, so did the need for the atrium. Churches built in the seventh and eighth centuries simply presented a flat, stark, boring facade to the street. To make the building look a little more interesting, church architects added square towers at one or both front corners. Because the flat tops of these towers often leaked when it rained or collapsed under the weight of snow, they began to be built with a pointed pyramidal top instead.

Now we're getting somewhere. (And note that the steeple caught on more in Germany, France, and England—countries with a cold climate and worse snow problems—than in sunny Italy, where churches with square towers continued to be built more frequently than elsewhere.)

These pyramidal caps, while tolerable enough on relatively small towers, looked positively ugly when they grew beyond a certain size. As bigger and bigger churches were built, with consequently bigger towers, designers looked for a prettier way to top them off. In about the thirteenth century, the octagonal spire was born.

But an octagonal spire on top of a square tower presents a problem of discontinuity where the two meet, which some critics considered ungraceful. So all sorts of turrets, dormer windows, gables, gargoyles, and other devices were added to camouflage the messy transition.

Another practical purpose of the steeple is to make the church easily identifiable, not only by worshippers trying to find it, but also by horseback riders in a steeplechase race, which originally was an obstacle race whose finish line was at a distant church whose steeple could be seen from far away. And the steeple often holds the church's bells. Nowadays, of course, a stranger in town can find a church by looking up its address in the telephone book, and most worshippers probably rely on their alarm clocks rather than the steeple's bells to get them to the church on time.

Even British church architect Peter Hammond, who considers steeples on modern churches a waste of money, admits that ''a soaring, aspiring tower, dominating the surrounding buildings, is an essential element in the *idea* of a church which has haunted the western European consciousness since the Middle Ages.''* Other architectural historians note Egyptian, Greek, Roman, Babylonian, and Mayan religious buildings also contained elements drawing the viewer's attention upward toward their gods in their heavens.

Nowadays, church architects often put steeples on churches for purely symbolic reasons. For example, Finnish architect Olav Hammarstrom designed a church in Wellfleet, Massachu-

---

* Peter Hammond, *Liturgy and Architecture* (London: Barrie and Rockliff, 1960).

setts, with a tower to make it visible not only from the land but also to sea travelers. This was not for practical reasons—the church doesn't have a dock for the use of passing vessels whose skippers might see the steeple and decide to drop in and pray—but is symbolic of the fact that the church is named after Saint James the Fisherman.

Can Flying Squirrels Really Fly?

* * *

It depends on your definition of fly. *Of course, they can't take off from* the ground and fly up into a tree, the way a bird can. But they can glide and land gracefully, while a person trying the same thing would just drop like a rock.

Flying squirrels can maneuver well enough in the air that you can play catch with them—and, unlike a baseball, they can play along. Scott Skinner, associate editor of *Wyoming Wildlife* magazine, recalled a childhood friend who kept a few of the rodents as pets. The whole family would don catchers' mitts and toss a squirrel around. The animals didn't seem to mind, he said. They would always make a perfect landing in the glove by using their tails and the sheets of membrane stretched between their hands and feet to "stall out" like an airplane and orient themselves. (In the wild, they do the same thing in order to land right side up on a tree trunk.)

Those membranes are called *patagia* (pat-A-gy-a), from the Latin word for the gold border on a Roman lady's tunic. Using its patagia and tail, the squirrel can steer its course while gliding up to two hundred feet at an angle of as little as 30 degrees from the horizontal. A more typical glide for the treetop-dwelling rodents is thirty feet, from tree to tree.

Flying squirrels are nocturnal, with large eyes that can see almost as well at night as those of an owl. They eat insects, nuts, buds, blossoms, and fruit. Sometimes they bury their food, as other squirrels do, but because they're not as nimble on the ground as they are in trees and in the air, they also store a lot of food in their nests. That's nests, plural. A single flying squirrel may have several addresses, each of them a hole in a dead tree, lined with shredded leaves, bark, and other padding.

They live in groups of twenty or more, and give birth in early spring to a litter of three or four young. Mother flying squirrels are very protective of their offspring. Loggers often notice flying squirrel nests in trees they've just cut down. If they pick up the babies, the mother will frequently come running to the rescue, climbing up the great big human being's pants leg to retrieve her children one at a time and take them to another nest.

* * *

How Do You Tell Mushrooms and Toadstools Apart?

* * *

*You don't. What you probably want to do is distinguish between poi-*sonous and nonpoisonous fungi. Although sometimes people use *toadstool* to mean a fungus that will kill you and *mushroom* to mean one that won't, this usage is not universal. Often the words are used interchangeably, though the practice of calling only the poisonous ones *toadstools* is over four hundred years old.

To avoid confusion, we could refer to them as ''edible'' versus ''poisonous'' mushrooms, but even that classification isn't altogether precise. Some people can eat large amounts of "poisonous" mushrooms and be fine, while others can get sick from what most people consider "edible" ones. And some mushrooms are perfectly safe for most people to eat, but contain a chemical similar to Antabuse, the drug some recovering alcoholics take to prevent themselves from drinking; you can get violently ill if you tipple within three days of eating these mushrooms.

There are many fungi, moreover, that are neither edible nor poisonous. They won't make you sick; they're just too yucky-tasting to eat. Giant puffballs, for instance (one of which con-

tains so many spores that if each one successfully grew to maturity, the earth would be covered in puffballs to a depth of eighteen feet).

As if the classification weren't confusing enough, the identification of different mushroom species isn't straightforward either. George Grimes, a mycologist (someone who studies fungi), says mushroom identification can be compared to telling the difference between lettuce and cabbage: It's hard to describe, but you know it when you see it. When picking wild mushrooms, he says, you must be certain of *all* factors necessary to the identification before you can be sure the fungi are safe to eat. Among the many characteristics you must take into account are: substrate (what the fungus grows on—soil, decaying wood, etc.); shape of the stipe (stalk) and pileus (cap); whether the cap is centered on the stalk; whether the stalk is hollow; texture of the cap (smooth, scaly, patchy, "hairy"); nearness to certain species of trees (with which some mushrooms have symbiotic, or mutually beneficial, relationships); shape and density of the gills under the cap (where spores are produced); and smell, color of fungus, and color of spores.

Grimes concludes that "there are no simple rules." If you want to gather wild mushrooms for your dinner table, go on field trips with a local mycological society, whose members can introduce you to one or two safe local species and warn you about deceptively similar-looking but poisonous ones. Once you're absolutely sure you can identify those, you can then gradually expand your culinary repertoire. "The only way to avoid trouble," writes mycologist G. C. Ainsworth, "is to profit by the past misfortunes of others and correctly identify species known to be harmless."*

---

* G. C. Ainsworth, *Introduction to. the History of Mycology* (Cambridge, England: Cambridge Univ. Press, 1976).

Even using a mushroom-identifying book won't necessarily protect you against poisoning. In 1988, two Californians ate some mushrooms identified as edible in a popular handbook, but the fungi made them so sick that they both required liver transplants. (They sued, but the courts ruled that the book's publisher was not liable.)

"It took a surprisingly long time before it was realized that there are no reliable rules by which poisonous species could be recognized," says one authority.* And it wasn't until 1847 that science recognized poisonous mushrooms as the exception rather than the rule. The ratio of safe to poisonous mushroom species is about the same as the ratio among green plants. Of the thousands of species of mushrooms, only about one hundred are poisonous, but only about one hundred others are edible and palatable. Even most of the poisonous species won't kill you, but will only make you get sick or hallucinate.

In ancient times, the Greek physician Galen warned his readers away from all fungi, though he admitted there were a few non-poisonous ones. The Romans had plenty of mistaken rules and tests for supposedly distinguishing safe from dangerous mushrooms, some of which persist today. For example, they thought it was safe to eat any mushroom that didn't blacken a piece of silver cooked with it, and that eating pears at the same meal with questionable fungi would protect them. Wealthy Romans loved mushrooms as much as other rare delicacies— both the benign (for their own dinner) and the poisonous (for feeding to their enemies). Nero became emperor after his predecessor Claudius had been dispatched by mushroom poisoning.

Modern medicine can save many victims of poisonous mush-

---

* W. P. K. Findlay, *Fungi: Folklore, Fiction, and Fact* (Eureka, Col: Mad River Press, 1982).

rooms today. But treatment of poisoning is at least as complicated as telling the bad fungi from the good. In many cases, symptoms don't appear until several hours after the tainted meal, so the patient may not even connect his illness with the fact that he ate mushrooms. Even if he does, he may not know what species it was, telling the doctor that he, like Alice in the Jefferson Airplane song, "just had some kind of mushroom." Bringing in specimens of the actual mushrooms may not be immediately helpful either, because most emergency-room staff are not experts in mycology.

Identification of the suspect mushroom is important, because different species contain different toxins requiring different treatments. One poison, amanitin, causes liver and kidney failure. (Specifically, it inhibits the transcription of DNA into messenger RNA.) Muscarine blurs the victim's vision, causes sweating, lowers blood pressure, and affects breathing; atropine is an antidote. Phalloidine is especially insidious, because after an initial phase of liver swelling, vomiting, and diarrhea, the patient appears to get better, but then the second phase of the poisoning hits, causing hepatitis and associated jaundice.

Typically, treatment for mushroom poisoning includes making the patient vomit (but avoiding dehydration, especially in children); giving activated charcoal to help prevent absorption of toxins by the body; antibiotics; and a low-protein diet. Other more controversial treatments include feeding the patient a goo made of the brains and stomachs of rabbits. (Some doctors think this might work because bunnies are immune to many poisons found in mushrooms, as are rats and toads.)

For hallucinogenic fungi like the Psilocybe species, the treatment is simpler, says mushroom-poisoning expert Kenneth Lampe. The effect wears off in about four hours, so just get a "sitter" to talk calmly to the person. In extreme cases, tranquilizers or anticonvulsant drugs may be useful.

We've focused on poisonous mushrooms, but a few centuries ago, people also searched for fungi that were thought to be positively beneficial. According to the sixteenth century European "doctrine of signatures," God had not only created medicinal plants, but had marked them with distinctive shapes or other signs to indicate what disease or body part they would be good for. Under this theory, the stinkhorn mushroom was classified as a remedy for infertility, not because of its horrid smell, but because of its shape. You don't need an illustration; you'll probably get the picture when you learn that its scientific name is *Phallus impudicus*.

What Is That Lump of Black Sludge You Sometimes Find in Oysters?

It's hard to imagine what prompted the first oyster consumer to conclude that the little geebers might be edible and were therefore worth a try. Perhaps some bony-browed Neanderthal with marginal eyesight and questionable judgment stepped on one along the shore, broke it open, and thought: "Hey, that gray, quivering, chunk of slimy tissue looks lovely!" *Glug!* As Jonathan Swift wrote in 1738, "He was a bold man that first eat [*sic*] an oyster."

I (Mark) never eat *raw* oysters, specifically because in their raw state they're in conflict with one of my dearest, most inviolable personal laws of conduct, namely: "Don't put it in your mouth if you're scared to touch it with your fingers!" Bruce, on the other hand, has been known to eat fifty of the things at one sitting, with Tabasco sauce.

One thing we've both noticed is that sometimes, if you cut an oyster in half, you'll find a lump of dark, sludgy, slightly gritty-looking material. Occasionally, it's so large and unappealing that the diner creates a final resting place for the oyster out of sight on the plate, under a lettuce leaf and pinned down by a crab-apple slice. We wanted to know what this stuff is, why its presence varies, and whether it's OK to scarf it down.

We got virtually no reply from the dozen or so oyster companies we wrote to (wonder why), but employees of various state and federal agencies were quite helpful. We contacted John Miescier, who works in the Shellfish Sanitation Branch of the Center for Food Safety and Applied Nutrition. He wrote:

> If your question relates to "black sludge" encountered when you cut open the shell and find it on or near the outside surface of the meat, the "sludge" probably represents sediment or mud associated with the muddy bottom habitat of the oyster.
>
> If your question relates to the "dollop of black sludge" found when the meat of an oyster is cut, then according to Mr. Jack L. Gaines, Biologist with our Northeast Technical Services Unit (NETSU), it probably represents partially digested food in the stomach and midgut of the oyster. This material consists primarily of diatoms and other planktonic organisms that the oyster utilizes as food. Essentially, the oyster feeds on these organisms by filtering or straining them out of surrounding seawater. They are then digested by a system of organs consisting of a mouth, a short esophagus, stomach, crystalline style sac, digestive diverticula, midgut, rectum and anus. [The crystalline style is a gelatinous rod that is slowly abraded, causing it to release digestive enzymes. The diverticula are blind digestive tubules where final digestion takes place.] The oyster is able to

sort through this filtered material and reject non-food materials such as suspended sediments.

The amount of "black sludge" found in individual oysters is a function of the animals' feeding activities which can be influenced by available food in the seawater as well as the amount of sediment that the oyster must reject.

This oyster food material is primarily of plant origin and is part of the reason why the oyster is considered to be a highly nutritious food source. However, it should be noted that, from a public health standpoint, individuals are cautioned to consume only those oysters and other bivalve molluscan shellfish which have been obtained from waters classified as approved for direct harvesting by State shellfish control authorities. The guidelines associated with such a classification are delineated in the National Shellfish Sanitation Program (NSSP) Manuals of Operation.

Finally, in a coup de grâce, Mr. Miescier describes "the black mud or 'blisters' found locally on the inside of some oyster shells. These are formed by boring polychaete worms. If ruptured during shucking they can produce muddy deposits."

We received a similar answer from Philip Kemp, Jr., with the Marine Advisory Services of the North Carolina Aquarium, but additionally, he solved a puzzle we hadn't actually posed. He wrote:

Another "mystery" more appropriately termed "myth" which I would not be surprised if you were asked is, "Aren't scallops really stamped out of sting ray wings?" The answer to this is of course, No! Scallops are all the same size because they are the adductor muscle of the shellfish and they are graded by size. The muscle fibers of sting rays extend in a horizontal fashion and those of a scallop in a vertical fashion. If you were to stamp scallops from sting rays, they would immediately fall apart. Lastly, I should say that certain sting rays if properly prepared are excellent and would be exceedingly ruined if they were stamped full of holes.

So we know the oyster's gut contains plankton and some silt, that the amount depends on how nutrient-rich and muddy its feeding ground is, and that the dark dollop you sometimes encounter won't hurt you. The natural ensuing question is: How does an oyster separate plankton from silt in order to digest it?

Oysters, clams, and mussels are bivalve mollusks, meaning that their shells consist of two halves joined by a flexible hinge. One of an oyster's half-shells is larger than the other in all dimensions. The oyster rests on it, operating the other shell as a lid, exposing the gills to seawater. All bivalves have an organ called the labial palps, which help sort plankton from sand grains in the incoming water. Mollusks in general tend to have sorting mechanisms throughout the digestive tract and on the gills. Some mollusks can discriminate several sizes of silt, and some can even modify the tolerance of a sorting surface by altering the surface's blood pressure. One sorting scheme involves a tissue surface with an alternating set of grooves and crests. The width of the grooves is wide enough for plankton to settle in them, but too narrow for sand. Cilia (very small hair-like structures) in the grooves beat continuously, pushing the plankton along the grooves toward the mouth. Cilia on the crests beat at right angles to the grooves, pushing the sand resting atop the crests toward expulsion.

A more serious issue is whether it is safe to eat *raw* shellfish. We received a lot of advice on this point from the Food and Drug Administration. Our short answer is: Maybe— assuming your immune system isn't compromised, you don't have certain ailments, you buy from reputable grocers, you discard suspicious shellfish, you refrigerate them properly, and you don't store them for long (unless frozen). Shellfish tend to concentrate, in their tissues, harmful bacteria, viruses, chemicals, and certain specific plankton-generated toxins, when present as feeding-ground contaminants, because they filter large amounts of water. (Oysters filter about four quarts an hour, clams filter three.) The National Shellfish Sanitation Program is the means by which the FDA monitors the safety of the 124 million pounds of bivalves harvested annually in the United States. This program oversees state shellfish programs.

State programs monitor shellfish beds, and shut them down when found to be contaminated. (Roadside shellfish purveyors should be avoided, because bootleggers will sometimes sneak into closed shellfish beds at night, and haul in the huge catches available there because of the harvesting ban!) State inspectors issue approval certificates to harvesting boats and shucking plants. These plants stamp an identifying code on each package of shellfish they ship, which verifies to retailers that their supplier has been certified, and assists in product recalls and the identification of contaminated feeding grounds. Nevertheless, participation in these programs is widespread but voluntary, and state-by-state inspection procedures vary. In early 1993, FDA commissioner David Kessler began a push to tighten seafood safety standards, citing a puzzling increase in food-borne illnesses (from seafood *and* nonseafood sources), resulting in an estimated nine thousand deaths a year.

A pamphlet of the Interstate Shellfish Sanitation Conference implores the following people to avoid raw or undercooked oysters (and, presumably, clams and mussels too):

* *Long-term alcohol abusers and people with liver disease.*
* *Patients with cancer, AIDS, diabetes, inflammatory bowel disease, or achlorhydria (a condition that reduces the presence of stomach acid).*
* *Patients using immunosuppressive drugs, or steroids for chronic conditions.*

The pamphlet also offers advice on the handling of oysters in the shell (which should be live). Oysters with shells that are broken, or that are agape and don't close tightly when tapped, that are dry, or that don't smell fresh and mild, should be thrown out. Oyster meat usually has a creamy tan color, but sometimes has a reddish or greenish tint that disappears with cooking. However, a pink oyster with a foul smell should be chucked, not shucked, since it has a yeast infection.

Some years ago, in response to a media brouhaha about seafood safety, the FDA conducted a study of the risk of illness from the consumption of various meats. At the time, the estimated illness rate for raw shellfish was one per thousand to two-thousand servings. For chicken, it was one per twenty-five-thousand servings, and for seafood (excluding undercooked shellfish), it was one per million. Raw shellfish accounted for 85 percent of all seafood-derived illnesses.

Louisiana requires the following warning at all shellfish outlets: RAW OYSTERS, RAW CLAMS, AND RAW MUSSELS CAN CAUSE SERIOUS ILLNESS IN PERSONS WITH LIVER, STOMACH, BLOOD, OR IMMUNE DISORDERS. California requires a similar notice on containers of oysters harvested in the Gulf of Mexico.

So what can you "catch" from shellfish and why?

Shellfish beds contaminated with sewage may contain the potentially fatal hepatitis A virus and cholera bacterium, and the Norwalk virus, which causes flu-like symptoms. States inspect for these hazards by testing shellfish beds for fecal-coliform bacteria, the presence of which implies sewage contamination.

Three forms of *vibrio* bacteria are ubiquitous, flourish in warmer waters, and cause gastroenteritis (including diarrhea and nausea). Vibrio vulnificus is of special concern because it kills an estimated 40 to 50 percent of the previously described at-risk individuals who contract it.

Perhaps more insidious are the illnesses caused by toxins produced in some algae blooms: the so-called red tides. Environmental changes such as water temperature increases and the upwelling of nutrients cause ever-present algae to bloom explosively, coloring the water (but not always red). If the algae include certain *dinoflagellates,* shellfish that consume them (especially mussels) can cause neurotoxic shellfish poisoning (NSP) or paralytic shellfish poisoning (PSP). (Dinoflagellates are single-celled creatures that are part plant, part animal. Like an animal, they eat solid food, and move about by wiggling two whip-like tails called flagella, but they also contain chlorophyll and can photosynthesize.) PSP takes thirty minutes or less to cause tingling, burning, or numbness in the face or mouth, which progresses to muscle weakness and paralysis, causing a medical emergency. NSP has somewhat similar but milder symptoms. Cooking does not neutralize the toxins. Shellfish inspectors regularly test susceptible waters for dinoflagellates, because they can contaminate the water for days before a bloom is visible. The way that most shellfish are tested directly for these and other toxic substances is by watching what happens when you inject mice with the ground-up meat!

Another algal menace is a species of diatom that secretes domoic acid, resulting in amnesic shellfish poisoning (ASP). The acid is an excitotoxin; it overstimulates and thereby kills nerve cells in the hippocampus region of the brain, and in so doing, cripples the victim's short-term memory.

There's an old saying that it's best to eat shellfish in months with an *r* in them. There may be some wisdom to this, since many of the contaminants discussed above tend to flourish in warmer temperatures, and the only months with no *r* in them are the warm months of May, June, July, and August.

So, are *raw* shellfish safe? You decide for yourself. All we're willing to say is that they're not as safe as betting on death and taxes, but they're unquestionably safer than juggling running chain saws in a room full of plutonium dust.

* * *

Are There Any Hiccup Remedies That Really Work?

* * *

Folklore is full of hiccup remedies. Many of them actually do work. No single method, however, works in every case. Some may be better than others for a given individual, depending on the cause and severity of the hiccups. A team of Saudi physicians wrote in a 1991 medical journal article, ''Perhaps there is no disease which has had more forms of treatment and fewer results from treatment than has persistent hiccup.''

Most mammals hiccup. Even fetuses hiccup, mostly in the

middle stages of pregnancy. Although it was once thought that
fetal hiccups helped the respiratory system develop, it's now
generally agreed that they serve little useful purpose either
before or after birth.

Although the length of an attack can vary, the mechanism is
consistent. The diaphragm lowers quickly, causing the lungs to
suck in air, but about one thirtieth of a second later the glottis
(area of the throat around vocal cords) closes, causing the
characteristic *hic* sound.

This process can go on for just a few hiccups or as much as
twenty-five years' worth. The causes, too, are varied, including
indigestion, swallowing air, sudden exposure to cold, and pregnancy. Anaesthetics used during outpatient medical procedures,
such as methohexitone, can induce hiccups. The Saudi doctors
quoted above had several patients whose hiccups were caused
by lesions in the part of the brain stem that controls breathing.
Anti-tubercular drugs cured them.

Sometimes the cause is psychological: anxiety and depression
after surgery, the suicide of a loved one, even job stress caused
by being passed over for a promotion. Psychologically induced
hiccups can be treated by hypnosis, by psychotherapy, and, in
one reported case, by the doctor offering the patient ten dollars
if he would hiccup just one more time!

Psychologist Monte Bobele, writing about hiccup treatment,*
theorized that treatments that don't work can start a vicious
cycle. The patient hiccups; friends recommend a folk remedy;
it doesn't work; the patient perceives this not as merely "not
getting better" but as "getting worse"; the psychological and
physical tensions that result then actually make the condition
worse. Bobele's article recommended that a hiccup sufferer's

* Monte Bobele, "Interactional Treatment of Intractable Hiccups," *Family Process*,
1989.

friends and medical caregivers refrain from pressing remedy after remedy on the patient, but rather, foster calmness and relaxation.

Still, Bobele and other hiccup researchers have collected many cures that have, at least on occasion, been shown to work. The ancient Greek doctor Hippocrates recommended sneezing. Even today, doctors sometimes tickle the nose or throat to induce sneezing, coughing, or vomiting to stop hiccups. Dr. Benjamin Spock says that babies' hiccups are often caused by swallowing air, so a simple burping often relieves them. Breathing air with a high (5 percent) concentration of carbon dioxide—the stuff you exhale, not the stuff that comes out of a car's exhaust!—frequently works. Recycling your breath in a paper (not plastic) bag accomplishes this.

Other hiccup cures that occasionally work include eating a teaspoon of sugar or some dry bread; drinking cold water or bicarbonate of soda in water; sucking on ice or a lemon; swallowing vinegar; pulling on the tongue or putting salt on it; scaring the victim; acupuncture; pressing on the eyelids; applying an ice pack to the back of the neck; pumping out the stomach; administering strong tranquilizers such as Thorazine; and cutting or anaesthetizing the phrenic nerve (which controls the diaphragm). Needless to say, don't try these last few at home!

How Were the Letters Chosen for the Game of Scrabble?

The Scrabble brand crossword game has enjoyed enormous popularity since its introduction in 1948. This game of 100 square tiles, each printed with a letter of the alphabet (except the two blank tiles, which are "wild-card" tiles), requires players to form words on the grid of 225 squares that constitute the game board, with the further requirement that each word formed (except the first, of course) must intersect with one or more words already on the board. Players score points by adding up the point values printed on the tiles played, and by applying double and triple bonuses for letters and words when a board square designated as such is filled.

Being curious about many aspects of the game and its history, we contacted Joe Edley, associate director of clubs and tournaments for the National Scrabble Association, and deluged him with the following questions:

Why does Scrabble have the distribution of letters that it has, and how were the letters' point values determined? In the Scrabble Tile Distribution Table below, the letters of the alphabet are given according to their frequency of occurrence in English, from most frequent to least, under the heading *Language Frequency*. The second column has them ordered by frequency of tiles in Scrabble, with quite a few frequency ties (such as A,I; and N,R,T). The last column gives tile point values. This table shows two interesting anomalies.

First of all, taking into account that many letters in the *Scrabble Frequency Count* column could be reordered with respect to other letters in the column with the same frequency, there are two letters whose frequency among Scrabble tiles is much different from their frequency in English: *H* (too infrequent) and *G* (too frequent). Why is this true?

Second, the point *value* of a tile is not consistently related to its frequency. Specifically, all letters with a frequency of 4 or more have a point value of 1, except *D,* whose value is 2! Also, half of the letters with a frequency of 2 are worth 3 points, the other half are worth 4 points! And finally, the five letters with a frequency of 1 have point values that range from 5 to 10! Why these inconsistencies?

Also, how were the dimensions of the board ($15 \times 15 = 225$ squares) and the number of tiles (100) decided? Where did the name *Scrabble* come from? What is the largest score a player can get with a single play? What are the two- to eight-letter words

✳ **Scrabble Tile Distribution Table** ✳

Language Frequency	SRABBLE Frequency Count	Point Value
E	E - 12	1
T	A - 9	1
A	I - 9	1
O	O - 8	1
I	N - 6	1
N	R - 6	1
S	T - 6	1
H	D - 4	2
R	L - 4	1
D	S - 4	1
L	U - 4	1
U	G - 3	2
C	B - 2	3
M	C - 2	3
P	F - 2	4
F	H - 2	4
Y	M - 2	3
W	P - 2	3
G	V - 2	4
B	W - 2	4
V	Y - 2	4
K	J - 1	8
J	K - 1	5
X	Q - 1	10
Z	X - 1	8
Q	Z - 1	10

that produce the highest scores, assuming no bonus points for anything? What are the rules for Scrabble tournaments, and is there a player-rating system as there is for chess? What is the highest score ever attained by a player in a Scrabble tournament, and what is done when a tournament game ends in a tie?

Mr. Edley's point-by-point letter response was very thorough:

> You asked several questions concerning Scrabble. Here are your answers.
>
> 1.   Alfred Butts chose to analyze a page of *The New York Times* to discover how to determine the frequency of letters for Scrabble. He simply counted the number of times each letter appeared on the chosen page. His guesswork is the basis for both the frequency and point values of the letters in Scrabble. Note that he only included 4 *S*'s in order to keep players from scoring too much by simply pluralizing words already played.
>
> 2.   We have no idea exactly how Alfred decided upon the dimensions 15 by 15.
>
> 3.   The name *Scrabble* was one of many names thought up by several people who were looking for a catchy brand name in 1948. Exactly who thought of it is currently unknown. It might well have been James Brunot, who marketed the game in 1948 through his ''Production and Marketing Company.''
>
> 4.   You asked what is the largest score a player could get with a single play, assuming that no more than one word is formed, and its maximum length is 8 letters. We also assume that you are asking for *acceptable* words only. And we also assume that you want us to use our current word source, the *Official Scrabble Players Dictionary*. Other dictionaries may lead to other high-single plays. We also assume that you are using only one regular set of 100 tiles. The answer is *OXAZEPAM* [a drug used to treat anxiety and alcohol withdrawal], which as a triple-triple [meaning that the word is played so that it covers two triple-word-score squares] can score $38 \times 9 = 342$ points $+ 50$

points = 392 points. [38 points for the letters, with the Z on a double-letter-score square. Multiply by 9 for the triple-triple, and add 50 points, which is the bonus for using all seven of the letters on a player's rack.] Of course, if the play is the last play of the game, then the player would also earn the points from his/her opponent's rack (doubled).

5.   Largest scoring two-letter word (LS2): JO or AX or EX or XI or OX or XU (all 9 points). LS3: ZAX (19 points). LS4: QUIZ (22 points). LS5: JAZZY (23 points) where one of the Z's is a blank. LS6: MUZJIK (28 points). LS7: MUZJIKS (29 points). LS8: SOVKHOZY (30 points).

[See below for the two-letter-words' definitions. The others: A zax is a tool for punching nail holes in roofing slate; a muzjik is a Russian peasant; and a sovkhozy is—or was—a state-owned Soviet farm.]

Here's one you didn't ask: What seven letter word can be spelled in Scrabble tiles that all have different values? JACK-DAW [—a common European bird similar to a crow and capable of mimicry]. One of the A's could be a blank with value zero.

6.   Enclosed are the 1993 Rules for National Scrabble Association Scrabble tournaments. However, we don't want them printed as is, since they are subject to change from year to year. If anyone asks, you can refer them to us.* In the same question you asked about our rating system. Yes, we have one, and it is computed similar to the chess system, though the numbers are different. The smallest ratings are around 200. The top-fifty rated players are rated from 1,940–2,091 currently.

7.   You asked: "What is the highest score ever attained by a player in a Scrabble tournament?" To us the question is incomplete. That's because there are several parameters. First, do you mean the highest single scoring play, or do you mean the highest total score for one whole game? In either case, Ameri-

---

* National Scrabble Association, P.O. Box 700, Greenport, NY 11944.

can Scrabble is very different from what the early British tournament Scrabble used to be like. The British used to play a variation of Scrabble called "High Score" Scrabble. In their version, the only goal was to score the most points, and each player would set up triple-triples throughout the game. By helping each other, the British regularly scored in the 600s and 700s. Their record is well over 1,000 points in one game. And their highest single play, we believe, was 392 points for CAZIQUES.

The British no longer or seldom use this "High Score" Scrabble as a regular format for their tournaments. They have recently adopted the American competitive version of play.

Our American Scrabble is to play to win. Scoring 285 points to 276 points is a win and just as valuable as winning 585 points to 576 points. The "spread" is the only important figure in our tournaments. That's how many points you win or lose by, and it's computed algebraically as positive or negative. Our system is much more competitive. What that means is that we seldom see scores into the 600s, because our players generally don't set up huge scoring opportunities. In fact, many of our players like to play very defensively, so that many times our experts don't even score 400 points.

With that in mind, our high single play is REEQUIPS for 302 points by Ron Manson of Toronto, and ANTIQUES for 293 points by Jack Eichenbaum of New York. Our highest one-game total was set by Mark Landsberg of Los Angeles early this year. He scored 770 points against Alan Stern, the highest-rated player at that tournament in Eagle Rock, California. Mark played five bingos (a bingo uses all seven letters of the rack, thereby earning an extra 50 points), including two triple-triples and one double-double. And, by the way, all words were acceptable. We don't count in the record books high-scoring games that have phony words played and unchallenged.

For tournament standings, a win is counted as one point, a tie as half a point, and a loss as zero points. So Player A earning 7 wins and 3 losses has the same win/loss record as Player

B, who has 6 wins, 2 ties, and 2 losses. In case of such a tie at the end of the tournament, the total spread is used to break the tie. The higher the spread, the higher the final placement in the tournament. In the previous example, if Player B with the 6 wins and 2 ties has a total spread of + 459 and Player A with 7 wins has a spread of + 343, Player B finishes higher.

The 1993 tournament rules that Mr. Edley sent us, which he insists are highly subject to change, are painstakingly thorough. Players follow a meticulous procedure when they wish to "challenge" the acceptability of a word played by an opponent. Challenges are processed by a Word Judge, and either fail or succeed, resulting in the loss of a turn by the challenger or challengee, respectively. The only acceptable alternative to the Official Scrabble Players Dictionary (OSPD) for the resolution of challenges (in 1993, at least), is Merriam-Webster's *Ninth New Collegiate Dictionary,* and *only* if the word exceeds eight letters in length and is *not* found in the OSPD.

The current rules encourage the use of smooth tiles, to prevent players from touch-sensing the tiles' letters when they draw them from the tile bag. Before the game, the tiles are counted and their letter distribution confirmed. The tops of tiles must always be visible to the opponent when placed on a player's rack.

Tournament games are timed using either Scrabble clocks, or sand timers. Clocks are preferred, track the elapsed time for each player during his turns, and are started and stopped as play moves from one opponent to the other. Players are allowed twenty-five minutes elapsed time per game. The penalty for exceeding this limit is to subtract ten points per excess minute or fraction thereof.

When three-minute sand timers are used, each player has three minutes per turn, and the game is stopped after fifty-four minutes, at which time each player is allowed one more play.

There are many error situations described, such as drawing new tiles out of turn, or failing to specify the letter represented by a blank tile. The latter situation is one in which the tournament director may assess a fifty-point penalty. Under no circumstances, however, is the assessment of a directorial penalty allowed to determine the ultimate winner of a game.

The rules even admonish players to avoid unethical behavior. Most of the examples given involve deliberately speaking to an opponent in such a way as to psych him out of issuing a challenge, or psyching him into a challenge that will fail.

There are 94 two-letter words that are acceptable in Scrabble. For all you budding Scrabble-philes, we've listed them below and footnoted their definitions (where not fairly well known).

✳ Legitimate Two-Letter Words for Use in Scrabble ✳

AA[1]	AD	AE[2]	AG[3]	AH
AI[4]	AL[5]	AM	AN	AR[6]
AS	AT	AW[7]	AX	AY[8]
BA[9]	BE	BI[10]	BO[11]	BY
DA[12]	DE[13]	DO	EF[14]	EH[15]
EL[16]	EM[17]	EN[18]	ER[19]	ES[20]
ET[21]	EX[22]	FA[23]	GO	HA
HE	HI	HM[24]	HO	ID[25]
IF	IN	IS	IT	JO[26]
KA[27]	LA[28]	LI[29]	LO[30]	MA
ME	MI	MM[32]	MO[33]	MU[34]
MY	NA[35]	NE[36]	NO	NU[37]
OD[38]	OE[39]	OF	OH	OM[40]
ON	OP[41]	OR	OS[42]	OW
OX	OY[43]	PA	PE[44]	PI
RE	SH[45]	SI[46]	SOP	TA[47]
TI[48]	TO	UH[49]	UN[50]	UP
US	UT[51]	WE	WO[52]	XI[53]
XU[54]	YA[55]	YE		

✳ **Definitions** ✳

1 A form of lava

2 One (Scottish origin)

3 Agricultural

4 A South American sloth with three toes on each foot

5 A small tree. Also called the Indian Mulberry

6 The letter *r*

7 An interjection (but *aw*, you knew that!)

8 Variation of *aye*, meaning *yes*

9 A bird with a human head, representing the soul in Egyptian religion

10 A sexual fence-straddler

11 Slang for *hobo*

12 Variation of *dada*

13 The letter *d*

14 The letter *f*

15 An interrogatory interjection (but you knew that, *eh?*)

16 The letter *l*

17 The letter *m*

18 The letter *n*

19 An interjection representing a pause in speech (but—er—you knew that)

20 The letter *s*

21 Regional slang—past tense of *eat*. (Jethro *et* all the possum gravy.)

22 Former spouse (arguably, the best kind)

23 Fourth note of the diatonic scale

24 An interjection expressing thoughtful contemplation

25 One of the three divisions of the psyche

26 Slang for *coffee*

27 The letter *k*—a variation of *kay*

28 Sixth note of the diatonic scale

29 A Chinese unit of distance, approximating one third of a mile

30 Third note of the diatonic scale

31 An interjection expressing satisfaction

32 Slang for *moment*

33 Twelfth letter of the Greek alphabet

34 Scottish-origin term meaning *no* or *by no means*

35 Means *born with the name* . . .

36 Thirteenth letter of the Greek alphabet

37 A hypothetical force believed by some in the mid-1800s to underlie all of nature

38 Variant of *oy*—a Scottish-origin noun meaning *a grandchild*

39 An interjection chanted in a Hindu mantra

40 Shortened form of Op Art—art involving optical illusions or ambiguities

41 A bone

42 See *OE*

43 The letter *p*

44 The principal word in a librarian's vocabulary

45 The seventh tone in the diatonic scale

46 The third letter of the Arabic alphabet

47 Same as *SI*

48 An interjection expressing hesitation

49 Same as *UH*

50 One (this is certainly a strange *un*)

51 A syllable sometimes used for the first note in the diatonic scale

52 Variant of *woe*

53 Fourteenth letter of the Greek alphabet

54 Vietnamese coin, one hundred of which equal currency called the dong

55 An interjection expressing disgust

Are Skunks Grossed Out by Their Own Smell?

Skunks may not smell good, but they smell well. That is, they have very sensitive noses, to make up for their poor eyesight, which has a range of only about three feet. They can definitely smell each other's spray: Biologist Vilis Nams of Nova Scotia Agricultural College told us how the skunks caged in his lab reacted as if in great danger when they smelled the dead skunk's scent gland he had brought into the room.

Skunks very rarely spray each other or anyone else. Nams

said he has captured dozens of skunks, and has never been sprayed, even while giving them tranquilizer injections, except once by some very young ones. Even then, he said, the mother skunk didn't spray to protect her young. Usually, when a skunk sensed that Nams was stalking it, it simply ran away as fast as it could, for up to half a mile.

In addition to running, skunks have several other defensive behaviors they use before going to the last resort of spraying. They fluff out their fur to make themselves look bigger, like an angry cat. They may do "handstands" on their front paws to display their distinctive striped or spotted fur as a warning to their attacker. They may also scrape their paws or stamp their feet on the ground as an auditory warning.

When all else fails, though, the skunk can shoot a stream of liquid stench as far as twelve feet. Humans can smell skunk spray up to two miles away. The scent of a spotted skunk lasts only a few hours, but that of a striped skunk may linger for two weeks.

Soap and water won't wash away the odor. In fact, the chemicals called thioacetates secreted by the scent gland react with water to form thiols, the chemicals that produce the smell. That's why a dog, sprayed by a skunk, may return to smelling normal after a few days, but has a relapse after jumping in a pond or getting rained on. Tomato juice is the traditional prescription for neutralizing skunk smell.

Perfume manufacturers have extracted some components of skunk juice for use in their products. Some people even like straight skunk odor. (It's thought that their noses have no receptors for the putrid chemicals in the mix.) There's a club for fanciers of the smell, through which aficionados can buy vials of liquid skunk essence and scratch-and-sniff cards. The pure stuff is also used as one ingredient in coyote-hunting lures.

Farmers tend to dislike the skunk, a member of the weasel

family. Although skunks keep the bug and rodent population down, they frequently carry rabies, and love to eat chickens. Two other words for skunk refer to this culinary preference: *Polecat* is a corruption of *poule-cat*—*poule* is French for chicken; *Zorrino* is the diminutive of Spanish *zorro*—a fox—another raider of henhouses.

Where's the Head in Headcheese?

*A*ll *over the place. There really is head in headcheese, and that's about* all there is; there's no cheese in it.

Here's how to make it from scratch, as described in the definitive cookbook by gourmet Craig Claiborne. Start with one pig's or calf's head. Then:

> *Have the butcher clean the head, removing the snout and reserving the tongue and brains. Scrub the head well and place in a deep kettle.*

Cover with equal parts water and wine . . . simmer very slowly until the meat is so tender that it falls easily from the bones. . . . Remove the root portion and skin from the tongue . . . lift the head onto a large platter. . . . Carefully remove all the rind from the head and cut the meat and tongue into pieces the size of large walnuts.*

Now take those brains you asked the butcher to reserve, cook them for fifteen minutes, then mix them with the head meat, tongue, and some seasonings. Pack all this stuff into a loaf pan, press it down with a weight, and let it jell in the refrigerator for at least two days. When done, it's shaped like a cheese, hence the name.

The meat-processing plants where headcheese is commercially manufactured employ a specialist known as a hog-head

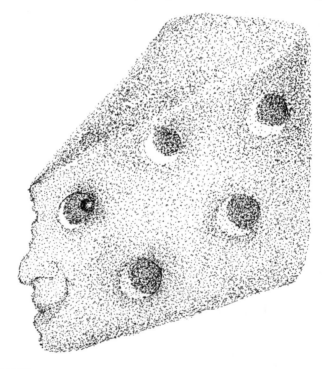

* Craig Claiborne, *New York Times Cookbook* (New York: Harper & Row, 1961).

singer. No, not a crooner like Frank Sinatra, but somebody who *singes,* or burns, the outside of hog heads. This honorable profession is officially described in the U.S. government's *Dictionary of Occupational Titles* as follows:

> 525.687-098 SINGER *(meat products). Singes hair from carcasses of suspended hogs to prepare them for further processing, using torch. Inserts end of butcher's steel into nostril of hog to remove hair. May be designated according to part of hog singed, as Hog-Head Singer.*

Nobody knows exactly who first made headcheese and where, but one dictionary says it seems to have originated in the American Middle West. The first known reference in print to headcheese appeared in a Virginia magazine in 1841. A century later, the *Saturday Evening Post* praised headcheese as follows:

> *The Pennsylvania Dutch are earthy. They see nothing wrong with calling something "head cheese" or "hog maw," and any outlander who can overcome a slight shuddering repugnance to taste them will wonder why he never even heard of such dishes before.* *

The article recommends eating headcheese chilled, sliced, and seasoned with vinegar or mustard. Or, for variety, it can be breaded and fried.

There are many other terms for headcheese, including "head pudding" and "hedge cheese." The *Dictionary of American Regional English* lists a second definition for headcheese: it's slang for *smegma.*

---

* Bill Wolf, "Eat Hearty, It's Plenty," *Saturday Evening Post,* Aug. 14, 1948.

Is There Really Any Such Thing As an Aphrodisiac?

*S*ure there is—if you define "aphrodisiac" cleverly enough. If you use it to mean substances that produce sexually related effects that can be measured in a laboratory, such as frequency of orgasm, length (in either sense) of erection, or physical endurance, then the answer is *yes*. It's also *yes* if "aphrodisiac" means a method of treating sexual dysfunctions. For example, four thousand years ago, Chinese doctors successfully gave testicular extracts to eunuchs to restore some of their male physical characteristics

and libido, according to Peter V. Taberner, author of a book*
on the long history of the search for aphrodisiacs.

If you use the word to mean something that increases sexual
pleasure, then again the answer is *yes,* provided you're willing
to accept subjective measurements of "pleasure" from people
who enjoy doing the horizontal bop under the influence of
Cuervo (and/or Acapulco) Gold. And, stretching it a bit further, you could even say that "aphrodisiacs" include products
intended to make you more attractive—if you accept, that is,
the advertising claims of (in descending order of believability)
exercise machines, clothes, cosmetics, automobiles, malt liquor, and cigarettes.

But (wink, wink, nudge, nudge) we know that the aphrodisiac everyone really wonders about is the magic potion that will
make that certain someone, who thinks you are a drooling clod,
fall madly in love (or at least fall into bed) with you. No, there
is no such thing as an aphrodisiac in this sense. But people have
been looking for it for thousands of years, and we doubt this
book is going to put a stop to that.

One of the most famous alleged aphrodisiacs is Spanish fly, or
cantharis, made from pulverized blister-beetles. To get some
idea of what this does when swallowed, consider that it was
used on the skin to form huge (twelve- by six-inch) blisters
deliberately, back when that was thought to be a good treatment for some diseases such as pleurisy, and even in modern
times has been used to dissolve warts. Taken internally, it
irritates the urinary tract. This may cause an itch that needs
scratching, but only in the literal sense.

Spanish fly is dangerous stuff. There are several cases in
British court records in which a Victorian seducer slipped his

* Peter V. Taberner, *Aphrodisiacs: The Science and the Myth* (Philadelphia: University
of Pennsylvania Press, 1985).

prospective conquest a potion containing cantharis, from which she later died or suffered serious injury. In one such case (*Regina* v. *Hennah,* 1877), the defendant was acquitted because it wasn't proved that he had intended to harm the victim.

Alcohol, considered as an aphrodisiac, has much more ambiguous effects. In moderate doses it may reduce premature ejaculation in men; have a mild anaesthetic effect, helping women who sometimes find intercourse painful; and reduce inhibitions in everyone, as demonstrated in the Flanders and Swann song in which another Victorian cad keeps urging his lady friend to "have some Madeira, m'dear!" But, as Macbeth's porter famously observed, the only three things that alcohol definitely produces are "nose-painting, sleep, and urine. Lechery," on the other hand, "it provokes, and unprovokes; it provokes the desire, but it takes away the performance"; it makes its victim "stand to, and not stand to." (Onstage, of course, this last line is usually accompanied by some predictable gestures with the porter's keys or walking stick.)

Ginseng, widely thought to have aphrodisiac and other healthful properties, is apparently more benign than alcohol, but doesn't seem to have any demonstrable effects on lovemaking other than pepping you up as caffeine does. Laboratory animals have been shown to have intercourse more frequently after ingesting ginseng, but as Peter Taberner points out, these results are hardly applicable to humans, for whom sex has overwhelmingly important emotional, social, and religious dimensions, rather than being mere instinct.

The *Kama Sutra,* the ancient Indian book on love, prescribes many aphrodisiacs containing highly nutritious foods as ingredients—for example, eggs, milk, and honey. In a civilization often faced with food shortages, such potions could, like caffeine or ginseng, help restore physical vigor. Even in the Western scientific medical tradition, as late as 1905, the authoritative *Merck Index* of medicines contained a section on aphrodisiacs.

Many of them were rich in vitamins, so they may have "worked" for the same reason (and to the same extent) as those in the *Kama Sutra*.

Rarity often enhances an item's reputation as an aphrodisiac. Europeans considered tomatoes and potatoes to be aphrodisiacs when the exotic plants were first brought from the Americas. If the thing is suggestively shaped as well as being rare or expensive, so much the better: The phallic vegetable asparagus, and powdered rhinocerous horn, are examples.

Both Asians and Europeans have taken the shape of an object into account when considering its usefulness as an aphrodisiac, a medicine, or a magic token. The medieval European "doctrine of signatures" held that God had indicated the usefulness of various plants by marking them in a way intelligible to humans. Thus, orchid tubers (which look like testicles) and carrot seeds (which grow into phallic-looking vegetables) were thought to be good male aphrodisiacs. Something that looked like a whole human body was thought to be a general tonic and cure-all: the mandrake root in Europe, and the ginseng root in Asia.

Less easy to explain are aphrodisiacs with disgusting ingredients. You'd think that these lotions and potions would repel, not attract, one's beloved. The *Natural History* of the Roman author Pliny contains, as Peter Taberner describes it, "a rich treasure of unpleasant marvels," including the right lobe of a vulture's lung, sewed up in a bag made of crane skin, to be tied onto the man's body. An Arab treatise called for a mixture containing magpie excrement to induce heterosexual lust in a woman, and for a preparation including burnt goat's hoof (and, among other things, *male* ferns) to excite lesbian ardor. The recipes in that book came with only a limited warranty, however: The pious author ended each prescription with the word *inshallah*—"God willing."

Did Cowcatchers on Trains Really Catch Cows?

Railroad cowcatchers—an inclined frame on the front of a locomotive—would more accurately be called cowtossers. They had two purposes: first, to prevent animals on the track from getting under the wheels and derailing the train; second, to avoid harming the animal, if possible.

Derailments of early railroad trains were so common that tickets often contained a clause requiring passengers to get out and help put the train back on the tracks in case of one. Cattle, hogs, and wagons on the tracks could all derail a train.

To prevent such accidents, American railroad pioneer Isaac Dripps invented the cowcatcher (sometimes called a cattle guard or a pilot). Dripps, of the Camden and Amboy Railroad, had first become well known in 1831, when he assembled the John Bull, a steam locomotive shipped from England in pieces, and made it run, even though he had never seen a train engine before. A couple of years later, he attached a plowlike wood-and-metal device to the front of the train. It extended farther in front of the engine than later models, so it had to have its own set of little wheels to support it. In 1838, British engineer David Stevenson (that's *engineer* as in "designs things," not "drives a train") described an encounter between this device and a wagonful of firewood that had been parked on the track: The wagon "was literally shivered to atoms by the concussion."

Stevenson told the folks back home in England about the cowcatcher because they had never seen one, and still hadn't even after the device had become universal on American trains in the 1850s. English railroads didn't need cowcatchers, because of a difference in American and English railroad law. In England, farmers were liable for damage caused by animals that wandered out onto the tracks, so they had an incentive to keep them fenced in. In America, however, railroads were liable to farmers whose livestock they killed, so American railroads had an incentive to move cows out of the way as gently as possible.

One early design for a cowcatcher, on the Philadelphia and Reading Railroad, consisted of parallel rods extending forward and downward from the front of the train. The idea was to scoop up and hold the cow until the train could be stopped, at which time, Bossie could be freed to get back to grazing. Unfortunately, the first animal this train ran into was a bull much bigger than the cowcatcher had been designed for. Instead of being gently held between the rods, it was impaled on them and killed. The shish kebab was stuck so firmly on the rods that it took a second locomotive to pull the carcass off.

Acknowledgments

We hope you've enjoyed this book, and we hope you'll join us in thanking the many people who helped make it possible by providing answers and pointing us to sources of information. Among those who kindly responded to our letters, telephone calls, and Internet inquiries were:

John Ahlnach, National Stuttering Project

Kim Badcock, CSIRO (Hobart, Tasmania); Judith Bagal, National Puzzlers League; Jim Ball, Dr Pepper/Seven-Up Companies, Inc.; Richard Banks, American Orinthologists' Union; Arlene Barnhart, National Fire Protection Association; Gabriel Baum; Allan Bell, Jr., Dektor Counterintelligence and Security, Inc.; Gale-Ann Bost, Hiram Walker and Sons Limited; Jorge Briozzo, SeaFest/JAC Creative Foods; L. Edwin Brown, American Culinary Federation, Inc.; John Buffalo, General Electric Railcar Services Inc., William R. Burk, University of North Carolina; Randy Buxton, Vendo Co.

Henry L. Canty, American Association of Police Polygraphists; Halbert Carmichael, Raleigh, NC; Manuel Carro, UPM; George Charalambous, Anheuser-Busch, Inc.; Joe Chew, Lawrence Berkeley Laboratory; George R. Cockle, Union Pacific Railway.

Bruce Davis, Academy of Motion Picture Arts and Sciences; Marshall Dermer, University of Wisconsin at Milwaukee; Charles C. Diggs, American Speech-Language-Hearing Association; Aileen A. Dullaghan, Food Marketing Institute; Gary Dunn, Young Entomologists' Society.

Brian H. Eckert, Wake Forest University; Joe Edley, National Scrabble Association; Anita Epstein, Associated Health Foundation, Inc.; Audrey Esquivel, USDA Office of the Consumer Advisor.

Ardie Ferrill, California Department of Food and Agriculture; Douglas P. Forsman, Oklahoma State University; Jane Fraser, Stuttering Foundation of America.

Pat Gandy, Seattle Institute for Sex Therapy, Education and Research; Marsha R. Gardner, Hershey Foods Corporation; Herbert G. Goldberg, Foundation for Fluency; Andrea Gosda, Whitehall Laboratories; Dharm Guruswamy, University of Maryland.

Ted L. Hake, Hake's Americana and Collectibles; Elizabeth Hall, American Red Cross; Jack Hanna, Columbus Zoo; W. Darryl Hansen, Entomological Society of America; Albert Harris, University of North Carolina at Chapel Hill; David Harrold, Milwaukee School of Engineering; Margaret H. Harter, Kinsey Institute for Research in Sex, Gender, and Reproduction; Ernest Hartmann, Tufts University School of Medicine; Neil Harvey, The International Academy for Child Brain Development; Jon Haugsand, University of Oslo; Richard D. Heffner, Motion Picture Association of America, Inc.; Janet Hinshaw, The Wilson Ornithological Society; Donna J. Holmes, University of Idaho; Horseless Carriage Club of America; Frank Horvath, Michigan State University; Steve Huberts, Model T Ford Club International; Robert P. Hymes, Columbia University.

Edgar Ingram, North Carolina Department of Agriculture.

Kevin R. Jones, University of Louisville; Jerry W. Jordak, Case Western Reserve University.

Roman Kaminski, International Fire Buff Associates; Allan Keith, American Birding Association; Philip S. Kemp, Jr., North Carolina Aquarium; Pablo Kleinman, University of Southern California; John Kolassa, University of Rochester.

Marcia Lane, American Association of Blood Banks; Chris Langston, Peoria Railway Historical Society; Herbert Lapidus,

Combe Inc.; Rae Larson, Seattle Institute for Sex Therapy, Education and Research; Cathleen R. Latendresse, Henry Ford Museum; Cynthia R. Levine, North Carolina State University; Jay Levine, North Carolina State University; Larry I. Lipshultz, Baylor College of Medicine; Gregory Lukow, American Film Institute; Peter Lund, Society of Fire Protection Engineers.

Jon Machtynger, Ingres U.K.; Walter O. MacIlvain, Veteran Motor Car Club of America; Elizabeth A. McMahan, Chapel Hill, NC; Gregory G. Mader, American Sleep Disorders Association; Jack L. Martin, Society of Automotive Historians; Ana Martinez-Holler, Hollywood Walk of Fame; Daniel Maye, International Association of Culinary Professionals; Roger L. Mayer, Turner Entertainment Co.; Robert L. Metcalf, University of Illinois at Urbana-Champaign; John J. Miescier, Center for Food and Safety and Applied Nutrition; Kim M. Miller, Antique Automobile Club of America; Joseph C. Mitchell, University of Richmond; Daniel P. Mullen, AIM USA.

Vilis Nams, Nova Scotia Agricultural College; Ed Noga, North Carolina State University College of Veterinary Medicine; Jennifer L. Northrop, United Fresh Fruit and Vegetable Association.

Barry O'Brien, Standard Change Makers, Inc.

Joseph Pawlik, University of North Carolina at Wilmington; J. Donlan Piedmont, Norfolk Southern Corporation; Stephen Potter, British Information Services; Bradley L. Pugh, Aladan Corporation.

David M. Reid, Raleigh, NC; Wade Rich, University of California at San Diego Medical Center.

Sarah K. Schneewind, Columbia University; John E. Simmons, American Association of Ichthyologists and Herpetologists; Madeleine E. Sloane, American Dehydrated Onion and Garlic Association; Frederick P. Smith, Jr., Institute of Makers of Explosives; Tom E. Smith, Food Lion Corporation; Chet Snouffer, United States Boomerang Association; Barzilai Spinak, Univerity of Maryland; Victor A. Sterner, ICI Explosives USA Inc.; Michael Stymac; Mel Sunquist, University of Florida.

Blair Tindall, Broadway musical *Miss Saigon;* Mel Turner, Duke University.

Richard Urena, University of Massachusetts.

Eddie Van Huffel; William T. Vetterling, Polaroid Corporation.

Charles Walcott, Cornell Laboratory of Orinthology; Todd C. Wehner, North Carolina State University; Evan Werkema, Case Western Reserve University; Chuck Westfall, Canon USA, Inc.; Jennifer A. Wundrock, Wisconsin Pharmacal Co., Inc.; Ann Wycherley, Royal Warrant Holders Association.

Anne York; Combe Inc.

As always, we offer our special gratitude to the staffs of the research libraries at the University of North Carolina at Chapel Hill, North Carolina State University, and Duke University.

Through gritted teeth we thank Phil "Careful with Those Diodes, Eugene" Gustafson, and Terry Chan, Chief Rabbi and Urban Legend Maven of the Lawrence Berkeley Laboratory, who found the one known error in our previous book, *Did*

Mowhawks Wear Mohawks? We had incorrectly written that urea is not found in the urine of any mammals other than human beings and Dalmatian dogs. In fact, urea is in just about every mammal's urine; it's uric acid that only you and I and those spotted mutts produce.

Phil and Terry get free copies of *How Does Olive Oil Lose Its Virginity?* as do these readers who sent in questions we answered in this book:

Morse F. Kalt and Christopher Trent Womble, who was five years old when he asked about elephant trunks.